I0762923

EVEN *the* DARKEST NIGHT

EVEN *the* DARKEST NIGHT

A FATHER'S JOURNEY
OF HOPE AND HEALING
FROM PATERNAL DEPRESSION

CHRISTOPHER G. CHOUKALAS, MD, MS

HARMONY

Harmony Books
An imprint of Random House
A division of Penguin Random House LLC
1745 Broadway, New York, NY 10019
harmonybooks.com | randomhousebooks.com
penguinrandomhouse.com

Library of Congress Cataloging-in-Publication Data is available upon request.
ISBN 978-0-593-98022-4
Ebook ISBN 978-0-593-98023-1

Printed in the United States of America on acid-free paper

1st Printing

First Edition

BOOK TEAM: Production editor: Andy Lefkowitz • Managing editor: Allison Fox • Production manager: Meghan O'Leary • Copy editor: Sue Warga • Proofreaders: Alissa Fitzgerald, Marcell Rosenblatt, and Megha Jain

Book design by Diane Hobbing

The authorized representative in the EU for product safety and compliance is Penguin Random House Ireland, Morrison Chambers, 32 Nassau Street, Dublin D02 YH68, Ireland. https://eu-contact.penguin.ie

To Lindsey, who saved my life

CONTENTS

INTRODUCTION

That you've never heard about paternal post-natal depression (PPND) before, much less read an entire book about it, is about to change. This book is the first to describe PPND, which I also refer to as simply paternal depression, but I am hardly the first man to suffer from it. Millions of men every year are so impaired during the transition to parenthood that they will lose out on weeks or months of bonding with their babies and supporting their spouses. That a name for my misery existed was the first sign of hope, and the signal that I might one day get better. And you've all heard the same tropes: Men don't talk about their feelings and men don't seek help. You've heard them because they are largely true, and this needs to change.

PPND is a mental health crisis that has not yet gotten out from under the stigma of men suffering from emotional problems and mental illness, and yet whenever I speak the words, use them out loud, from a deep well of personal experience, I universally hear some version of "This is hiding in plain sight and nobody is talking about it." New fathers are suffering, and they're not talking about it or getting help. Wherever we are on the spectrum of progressive thoughts about men having needs and needing help with emotional problems or mental health, if there was ever a time when men *really* weren't supposed to have needs, it is after their partner gives birth to their children. And yet it is a time of immense change for fathers, too, who experience grief around the loss of a prior identity, unpredictable hormonal changes that affect mood and behavior, and often a new dual expectation of supporting a family in all the traditional ways while becoming emotionally available to a new life-form, one that early on is more akin to an alien being speaking a different language than a beloved offspring with whom we are able to bond.

And that's if everything goes smoothly; throw in a birth trauma here or a congenital illness there, and you've got the makings of a sick dad who doesn't even know it, one who acts like a belligerent, selfish jerk, and everyone wonders why. I have heard some version of "I think my husband had that" or "Maybe that's why I was so irritable all the time" too many times not to take my own grief, my own suffering, and put pen to paper.

I don't know exactly where or when it started, this thing we call my anxiety, or my paternal post-natal depression. I guess the further back you look, the further back it appears. That first week home with the girls, I kept an elaborate spreadsheet of all their ins and outs: each wake cycle, each feeding, down to the minute, each poop, each heavy wet diaper (did I weigh them? I did not, but home scales exist, and I might have if I had had one). These numbers were dutifully recorded, with formulas that calculated totals for graphing purposes. I am an intensive care physician, and it seemed important to know if they were drinking enough. Was it over the top?

If it was, it didn't end there. Was it their crying in the night, the unpredictability of it? Or did the crying itself do something else to me, triggering something deep down within me about my own childhood? Was it birth trauma? Did watching my wife, Lindsey, bleed nearly to death set the stage? Did the hours and days contemplating life with an intensive-care patient for a wife—or, worse, becoming a widower father—unhinge me in some fundamental way? Loosen some thread that was just barely holding me together in easier times? Or was it later, when my daughter Pia started having all those fevers? They'd be 103 degrees for days at a time, with no cough or cold, no gastrointestinal symptoms, nothing to say she'd merely caught some virus, something that would be pretty normal at that age. Was it cancer? Something worse?

The truth is, I don't remember a time in the girls' early lives when I didn't feel waves of panic coursing through my body. My feelings were a result of all these things and more, going back to before I was born, not just to the way I was parented but also to how my parents and probably *their* parents were parented. Or maybe I was always anxious. Maybe the importance of control was just a balancing act, just the view from below a hundred spinning plates, the kind a child like I'd been couldn't let fall. The cycle breaks with me, though, and the process of writing this book, of recovering from my depression and anxiety, of examining and challenging what was meaningful to me, good or bad, in the years I've lived, is at least in part so I can parent my own children in a way that, with any luck, leaves them more whole than I was when they were born.

As an anesthesiologist and intensive care physician at the University of California, San Francisco, during the height of the COVID pandemic, I saw unthinkable physical and emotional tragedies at my job every day, from seeing three generations of a family perishing in less than a month, to COVID patients crying to just be touched. And yet these horrors were light-years easier to bear than caring for my infant twins.

There were a million reasons not to write this book, a million reasons not to expose myself and my family to having outsiders know and pass judgment about what we were going through. I am, at heart, a stoic Midwesterner who at first maybe didn't believe I actually had a mental illness, who believed that maybe I was just a selfish, angry person who couldn't get on board with what it took to be a loving and effective parent and partner. What would people think of me as a person, a man, as a physician, if I revealed so much vulnerability and weakness? "My wife went through fertility treatment, too; we had twins, too; I was fine," some might say. "What's wrong with you?" Hearing that, I might agree that something unfixable was wrong with me, and shrink back inside myself. I was also acutely aware that because I am a man, elevating my experience of depression and anxiety that occurs after becoming a parent, something that has heretofore been a woman's story to tell, could generate some blowback. But I hope there is enough space to talk, to have an open dialogue about PPND and bring it to greater awareness.

My parents, or at least my mother, did the best they could with the hand they were dealt. That it wasn't enough of what I needed in order to have my head screwed on tight is on display in the pages that follow. My upbringing was marked not by confidence and material ease, but in part by my mother's own struggles. Beyond historical accuracy, beyond the need to try to make sense of my own story and develop some explanation for what happened, what is her role in all this and is it fair to expose that to the world? I know she will hear some of what I remember, some of what I write, as judgment. As blame. My life moving forward might have been easier without all of that.

And what of my girls? What would they think later in life, should anyone actually read this thing and keep it alive in the cultural consciousness until they are old enough to realize themselves what I went through when they were born? I've wondered at many early points in their lives if they could somehow sense my suffering. Like, could they hear in my voice or feel in my touch that I didn't know how to love them or bond with them, or that the sound of their cries, the expression of their needs, would send me into a tailspin of anxiety and fear? At age five, they are so extraordinarily joyful and resilient that I have put to bed those worries about them having sensed it as babies. But a book is different, and they'd be old enough to be aware of it, what it's about. Would they feel responsible? What burden would this place on them? Would they worry I resented them? Feared them? Or is the lesson for them in all of this that at least I was strong enough to get help?

I was also told by some very smart people that "men won't have the insight to recognize themselves in this." But I have consistently found this to be false. Men, when given permission to feel and talk, will do so, and once they start, they may not stop. By standing in the presence of another man and opening the door to vulnerability about the kinds of things men feel when they become parents, even under the best of circumstances, men will share the rich inner world of their feelings, experiencing an entirely new form of intimacy.

In the end, I didn't really have a choice but to write this; it simply exploded onto the page, at times like a bomb. That so many men seem to have suffered in silence, without a voice or sense that the pain they were living had a name and could be made better, propelled me forward and out of the shadows. My hope is that by doing so, men will see themselves in these pages and know they are not to blame for their feelings and fears, that there is help, that they don't have to feel as awful as I did, and that they can get better.

EVEN *the* DARKEST NIGHT

CHAPTER 1

THE DARK AT THE END OF THE TUNNEL

OUR ANESTHESIOLOGIST, DR. Oana Maties, probably didn't know why she dreamed of death the night before our twins were born. Nor, wisely, did she tell us beforehand. But there was something in the way she lingered a beat too long on the one small part of her consent paperwork—Lindsey's consent to receive donated blood. Maybe that didn't reach my consciousness, at least not right away, but it set off a subtle alarm bell, an annoyance almost. *Geez,* I thought, *I've done anesthesia for hundreds of cesarean sections and never focused on blood this much.*

As an academic anesthesiologist and intensive care physician, a physician who takes care of patients in the operating rooms and Intensive Care Unit at the University of California, San Francisco (UCSF), I've had versions of that talk with my own patients thousands of times. The thick stack of preoperative paperwork had become second nature to me in my own practice. Her perseveration was subtle, but unmistakable all the same. The paperwork was completed in a matter of minutes, but what lingered was my colleague's pause as she hovered over that medical release, the soft catch of concern in her voice, the undercurrent of foreboding.

A premonition of death is a very unusual thing for any doctor to admit, let alone an anesthesiologist at an elite academic university. It's squishy. Imprecise. Inconvenient. Unquantifiable against the backdrop of science that underpins our practice. Our belief in the knowable, the provable, the demonstrable is kind of a funny crutch that we use, an object of faith that allows us to do the things we do to patients, the risks we take. She couldn't have known this routine operation would be complicated; that my wife, Lindsey, would nearly die, bleeding so much and so quickly that her body would go into shock, not able to support enough blood pressure to remain conscious. None of us knew. And yet Dr. Maties paused there.

Lindsey had had a textbook pregnancy, which is very surprising because she was thirty-nine years old and carrying twins that were conceived via IVF after five and a half years of seeing countless doctors and specialists. The chances of her having a normal pregnancy after IVF was only about 20 percent, and that was for a singleton, not twins; plus, after all the failed cycles we'd had, who knew? In fact, her own obstetrician was scanning her chart toward the end of her pregnancy, asking what exactly the problem had been for those five and a half years when we couldn't conceive. As a fellow physician, I knew she wasn't so much asking what the diagnosis was (as with the majority of infertility cases, our formal diagnosis was "unexplained subfertility," and we would never have a clear answer about what was actually "wrong"); rather, it was a rare moment of candor in which she was essentially saying out loud, *I can't believe you are this far along without any complications.*

Lindsey ended up carrying twins to almost forty weeks. Between thirty-seven and thirty-eight weeks is considered to be full term for twins, and doctors often advocate for inducing birth at that stage. But the twins' conception was so heavily medicalized, her pregnancy was so filled with tests, procedures, and ultrasounds, that I am sure a part of her wanted the birth to be less like that. By the time we went to the hospital, on the morning of August 27, 2020, deep into the pandemic culture of shutdowns and social isolation, still months before the vaccine would give us some relief, it was almost painful for me to look at Lindsey because her belly was so huge. Even she would laugh and agree with this statement. She's five foot three with a petite frame, and from behind you couldn't even tell she was pregnant. I once heard someone standing behind her in line at the grocery store gasp when Lindsey turned around, "Oh my

God, she's *pregnant*!" The twins would end up being almost six and a half pounds each, a staggering combined thirteen pounds of baby on that tiny frame.

In the inky blue hours, just before sunrise, Lindsey woke me up gently to tell me that she felt she needed to go to the hospital. It had been too long, she said, and she didn't feel like she should be pregnant anymore. It was just a gut instinct, she said. We had walked five miles the day before along Crissy Field, one of the most beautiful open spaces in the city, under the splendor of the Golden Gate Bridge, the burnished red arches overhead, San Francisco Bay lapping beside us, the surfers daring to ride the waves in that notoriously complicated cove. Women smiled at her. I caught men eyeing her, even at almost forty weeks. She's just one of those women.

So there I was, at five in the morning, still groggy from sleep, still unsure what all was happening, still maybe buried in denial that these babies were coming at all, when Lindsey told me her mom, Ayn (pronounced "Ann"), was already driving into San Francisco, where we lived, from Marin County, where Lindsey grew up. Ayn would be our "lay doula," the only non-medical person allowed to be with us in the hospital at the pre-vaccine height of the COVID pandemic.

As Lindsey was telling me all of this, I recall thinking she was beautiful and that I should have felt like the luckiest guy in the world, overwhelmed with anticipation and excitement to meet our babies, for whom we had not just waited but also endured and suffered for so long. While I remember *thinking* that, I *felt* nothing—nothing for her, nothing for our unborn babies—and I'm not sure I realized it at the time. All the words and expressions that conjure up my state in that moment—empty, hollow, a robot—now sound clichéd and tired, but they were deeply true. I was a shell. I had spent most of my life "compartmentalizing," mentally separating hard or unpleasant things from my everyday internal dialogue, both because of my career and my own complicated childhood, but this had reached its zenith in the last nine months. I hoped no one had noticed, but I was checked out and disengaged from Lindsey and the entire pregnancy. In that moment, though, the reality of what was to come was just beginning to set in. All my mechanisms that kept my life orderly, that shielded me from uncertainty, from pain I didn't even know I had, would be dismantled, and I would find myself adrift—and I wouldn't even see it coming.

I don't recall what I was thinking as we drove to the hospital that morning to give birth. The three of us were huddled in Ayn's Volvo station wagon in the dark, early hours of the morning. The fact that I don't remember what I was thinking as I was about to meet my babies is telling in its own right: I'm always cogitating, thinking about next steps, obstacles, and work-arounds.

Our labor experience was a thirty-six-hour hellscape of sleep deprivation, confusion, and failure. Nothing seemed to stimulate Lindsey to have contractions, and one of the babies was moving around so much that the monitors, necessary to track fetal heart rate as a proxy for the babies' well-being, simply couldn't track her. The physicians and nurses spent literally hours at a time, all day and all night, adjusting this, moving that, trying to keep Baby B on the monitor, keeping us awake and miserable, and all the while, nary a contraction nor any sign of labor occurred. As our second day was turning to night, Ayn napped on the daybed under the long stretch of windows facing Oakland and the East Bay. The smell of smoke was just beginning to permeate the hospital; it would be another week until the Tubbs fire in Santa Rosa would cause the daytime sky to turn an eerie orange, something so bizarre news outlets throughout the world reported on it.

But for now, it strangely felt like we were camping and Ayn had come over to join us at the campfire, even as the trio of medical professionals huddled in the corner of the room tried to figure out next steps for Lindsey's induction. Ayn had birthed Lindsey's sister at home, unmedicated, in less than two hours. Lindsey was born in five hours. Ayn was a bit crunchy, an earth mom, favoring tinctures, whole foods as medicine, and yoga over antibiotics or even Tylenol. We'd often clash, me rolling my eyes at her severely unscientific approach to nearly everything. I'd rib her pretty hard about what I'd call "elephant placenta" (her favorite garlic and echinacea blend, which she swore by during flu season) or her faith in astrology over the scientific method as a way to make sense of the world. So imagine my shock when, in the middle of the hemming and hawing about next steps, she said, with the clarity of a phonograph needle scratching into silence, "I think we need to be talking about a C-section."

The physicians resisted, insisting that laboring to birth twins was still possible, still preferred, if only they could kick the induction into a higher gear. "Higher gear?" she scoffed. "We already can't monitor the babies, and you want to start a more dangerous medication that makes monitoring even more important? No, we need to get real and get these babies out." Ayn's logic was unassailable, the clarity and conviction undeniable, and Lindsey agreed with her. At this point we had tried a handful of things to stimulate labor and there wasn't a single contraction. It was strange. I'd had almost no sleep in thirty-six hours, but I remember being surprised and confused that the obstetricians, who typically love to do surgery, were trying to talk us out of a surgical delivery, while Lindsey and her mom, anti–conventional medicine as they are, couldn't have been more certain that surgery was the safest next step. What did I think of all this? I remember feeling helpless to intervene. Ayn's logic made sense, and to be honest, most twins are born by C-section anyway, so on some level I'd thought we'd end up here one way or another. Still, I think the physicians were looking to me to compel Lindsey and Ayn, and Lindsey and Ayn were looking to me to compel the physicians.

The sun was dropping, and shift changes were occurring for the third time since we had arrived two days earlier. Dr. Maties was crossing over the Bay Bridge from the East Bay and descending into San Francisco at that moment, her sense of unease just setting in as she walked into the front door of UCSF's Mission Bay Campus, the bright and shining crown jewel of the hospital's sprawling system. We had a younger obstetrician on call that day and night, Dr. Kiran Kavipurapu (Dr. Kavi, for short), who was telling us he had recently moved here from San Diego, hoping to live the storied Bay Area life, rich in outdoor activities, colorful political discussions in beatnik cafes, and, of course, the elusive yet alluring promise of being able to ski and surf on the same day. Instead he found himself in the thick of a pandemic lockdown, with restaurants, museums, and office buildings shuttered all around him. "Only hospitals are still open," he said, with a hint of humor. He was young, enthusiastic, and open-minded. A fresh mind, I liked him immediately, even in our agonizing state. We all did. It's a rare person who can work well with three different and disparate minds—my own, Lindsey's, and her mom's—and I will forever be thankful to him for this.

Oblivious to the swirl of physicians and nurses drifting in and out of the room, preparing this, checking on that, Lindsey leaned over, took my hand, and asked for her makeup. I laughed a little, charmed by her, as always. She wanted to make sure she looked cute in that first photo with our babies, even though she'd be covered in a sheet, swathed in a hospital gown, and wearing the blue bonnet, the one that means you're the patient in an operating room (OR). I handed her the makeup bag, and she tossed it to her mom as they wheeled her off. I can't recall if we said a prayer or huddled for one last moment or even made any phone calls. The distance from our room to the operating room could be covered in less than a minute. I could tell Lindsey was excited; she had always wanted to be a mom. I was terrified, almost to the point of vomiting.

When Lindsey first got pregnant, my close friend from college, Greg, and his wife, Lauren, had sent me a book on fatherhood. Greg had had an upbringing similar to my own, and I don't know exactly how he felt about becoming a father, but if you had asked me at the time, I think I envisioned our parenting dynamic like theirs: me going along for the ride and it mostly working out well. The book sat on my bedside table, untouched, for all of Lindsey's pregnancy. During our courtship, Lindsey had been clear from the get-go that she wanted to be a parent. I said I did, too, knowing that's what a normal person would say and what she wanted to hear. However, if you had asked me what kind of dad I wanted to be, or what values were important to me, or even what basic activities I would enjoy doing with my children, I would have stammered and come back with nothing. But as Lindsey was taken away to the operating room, everything I had pushed out of my mind for the last nine months—perhaps the last however many years—was now surging forward, pulsing, toward this new life . . . a life I couldn't control.

After they took Lindsey out, I waited in the hallway until the medical team could be sure the epidural was effective enough for the surgery, at which point they'd come get me. It was one of the few moments in the last thirty-six hours when I was alone, when I could think. After a certain amount of time I realized I'd been waiting too long. The cogitating side of me—the one thinking about the plan and the obstacles and the work-arounds—knew she had had an epidural placed hours ago and knew roughly how long it took to dose it for a C-section. All this was pushing to the side any other thoughts or feelings I might have had about what was to come.

Eventually, I was escorted into the room, the kind of room I'd walked into thousands of times as a practitioner. But this time it was not my room; I was a guest here, a civilian. I sat down on the stool meant for the non-birthing parent, just off Lindsey's left shoulder, and waited. Lindsey seemed kind of sleepy to me, but it had been a long time since she'd been able to rest.

"Uterine," I heard Dr. Kavi shout.

"Nine twenty," someone replied.

"Baby A!" he said.

"Nine twenty-one."

I stood up to watch as he pulled our first child out of Lindsey and held it up.

The calls "Baby B!" and "Nine twenty-four" came next, and the babies were whisked off to the waiting team of pediatricians and nurses in the room before I could get a good look at them, even before I could tell whether they were boys or girls (we hadn't wanted to know in advance). A few minutes later, one of the nurses asked me to come over to the bassinets and trim the umbilical cords, a tradition that I guess makes the other parent feel like they're necessary in the room. That's when I learned both the children were girls. I remember being glad they were girls. The only thing I can really remember from Lindsey's pregnancy was that I had hoped not to have boys. I wasn't exactly sure why; I've always said I just like girl energy. But maybe it was something deeper, like being estranged from my own father for so many years. Would I have known how to relate to sons?

Someone handed me the babies. Were they crying? Squirming? I couldn't for the life of me tell you. They were red, or pink I guess, and warm, with smooshed faces, and they were wrapped in those multicolored baby blankets that somehow seem to be the same at every hospital. They didn't move a lot, or maybe they couldn't, burrito-wrapped as they were in what I later learned was a swaddle. One of them (we didn't have names yet, but it was Baby A, the first one to come out) had a red, blotchy, heart-shaped mark on her forehead. "Just a stork bite," the nurse was quick to say, as if calling it a "stork bite" instead of using the medical term would be the least bit reassuring to someone like me. But I hadn't noticed the mark; I couldn't have noticed. It was all such a blur, a swirl of confusion, but for me it was all cognitive, not feeling. Not yet. What should a man feel when holding his twin daughters for the first time? How had my own father, absent most of my life, felt when I was born? How should he have felt? Full of pride? Joyful? Relieved? Terrified? Had he felt an instant bond, that Hallmark emotion where everything clicks into place the second a parent lays eyes on their newborn? Whatever it was I was supposed to feel, I didn't feel it. Those first moments are lost to me; the emotions, if I had any, were ephemeral, either because of all that swirled around me or because this was the beginning of all that would soon swirl within me.

What I do remember is seeing Lindsey's blood pressure on the monitor, just out of the corner of my eye, and knowing on some level—maybe in my gut, or in the animal part of the brain where instinct lives, but barely breaking into the realm of consciousness—that she was in trouble. Normal blood pressure is 120/70; 80/40 is suboptimal; 60/30, which is what Lindsey's was at that moment, is a life-and-death situation. In the back of my brain, behind all that was so overwhelming about holding the girls, I went through a series of scenarios to try to figure out why Lindsey's blood pressure was so low. The epidural dosing, maybe, or a "high" spinal, or maybe a little bleeding . . . something that would be minor, normal, fixable. I was sure it'd come up to a more normal level soon.

But as the minutes passed, the number remained stuck, red, blinking, and ominous. Like the nervous flyer that I am, I watched those in charge—Dr. Maties, Dr. Kavi, the nurses—the way I'd watch flight attendants in the middle of turbulence. They didn't look worried. They seemed to be following routine. They were smiling (they were, weren't they?), they were taking pictures of the girls with my phone, they weren't rushing around, so it must be okay. Right?

The whole thing was bewildering, absolutely bewildering. There I was in a busy operating room where the medical personnel seemed to be behaving as though things were going exactly right, and they'd thrust these two babies into my arms, and I was trying to figure out if my wife's blood pressure was good enough. The chaos of a busy operating room, of having a life (or two, or ten) intimately depend on my presence, is not new to me. And yet the very real dependence fostered by actually holding my daughters was something else altogether. At some point, amid the beeps and clicks and buzzes, amid what began to be slightly raised voices and an undercurrent of concern, someone took a picture of me with the girls, the very first one. I must have been holding them this entire time, standing there in the middle of the swirl of activity. It was about then that I saw that the syringes, the ones full of emergency medicines to raise the blood pressure, were nearly empty, and yet the monitor continued to show a blood pressure of 60/30. Then my ears began to register the voices in the room.

"Methergine!"

"Hemabate!"

"The pit's running, right?"

Then:

"Another Hemabate!"

"Can we give some more Methergine?"

"Give me some Pitocin for intrauterine injection."

These are all the names of medicines we give to make the uterus contract; after a C-section, without contraction the open veins of the uterus will gush blood, uncontrolled, out into the world. The same enormous blood supply that feeds those babies in utero, if left unchecked in a uterus that doesn't contract, will end up on the floor in minutes after the babies are out. Worldwide, hemorrhage from a uterus that doesn't contract is the leading cause of maternal death, and here we were, living it. The fact that these names were being called repeatedly meant the drugs weren't working, that people were running out of options, that they were getting nervous.

I called out to Lindsey, trying to show her the babies (she didn't want to know right away what their sex was): "Here are the gir—the babies, lovie!"

Nothing. Her eyes were closed, her forehead sweaty. The red blood pressure number was still 60/30. She'd waited her whole life to see these babies, but at that moment all I could see were the syringes. The purple ones. The ones I knew by heart. The ones that are supposed to reverse course when things go south.

The voices came again, closer to me, and louder this time, more hurried.

"Tell the blood bank to send O-neg instead."

"We need to enact the massive transfusion protocol; bring the Belmont!"

She was bleeding, too much, and it wasn't stopping. They needed the Belmont, a machine that helps warm and pump huge quantities of blood into a patient, and they didn't have time to wait for blood that had been cross-matched, checked against her blood for incompatibility, so they were giving the emergency blood, the stuff you give only when someone's bleeding to death. Because this *was* an emergency. Because she *was* bleeding to death.

The red number, still 60/30 . . .

I was still holding these babies like a sap, like nothing was happening, and no one was saying anything was wrong. But I knew. I'd seen patients with sweaty brows, ashen skin, gray lips, and fading consciousness before. And I knew what "bring the Belmont" and "send the O-neg instead" meant. I've called those same plays dozens of times, and they're pure defense, meant only to stem the tide when something truly heroic needs to be done.

The cooler from the blood bank arrived almost instantaneously. A cooler I've opened dozens of times myself, desperate for the blood it carries, meant to sustain a life for at least a little longer. The next thing I remember was seeing the blood, in all its greasy redness, coursing through heated tubing on its way to the large-bore IV in Lindsey's left hand, the IV put in hastily under the drapes, the one with the tape that wouldn't stick to her sweaty skin. My brain stem knew what this meant before my cortex did. Her body was so stressed from the blood loss that her brain wasn't working and her sympathetic nervous system, the part of our nervous system that makes us afraid, that helps us flee from danger, was pushing out sweat as fast as it could. To see her covered in sweat was both medically so disturbing to me and personally so absolutely foreign that in the moment I felt like I was looking at a stranger's body, not Lindsey's. It was like my brain was already distancing itself from what was happening, protecting me from what I knew was coming: death.

At that point I looked over the drapes and saw what looked like a giant beach ball on Lindsey's lap. Dr. Kavi had "externalized" Lindsey's uterus, taken it partially out of her body through the cesarian incision, to address the bleeding, and it was clear to me it was not contracting, which explained everything else we were seeing. I kept experiencing a disconnect between what was happening in me and what was happening around me. What I was seeing gnawed at my gut, or somewhere above my gut, but that feeling couldn't find a way out as words; it kept getting stuck, it wouldn't translate into action. I was in an OR, where I was usually the action, the pointy end of the spear, using my hands and my mind to do the work of rescuing a dying patient, but this time I was struck dumb. I was still holding those babies, and it wasn't my case, it wasn't my patient; it was my *wife*. I thought, *They wouldn't let me keep holding the babies if something was wrong, would they?* Anything to believe it was okay. But for that to be true, I'd have to deny everything right in front of my own eyes.

"Look at me. *Look at me,*" Dr. Maties shouted to me, snapping me out of what must have looked like a daze. "I know what you're thinking. Tell me what you're thinking. Tell me where you're going. We're not going there. We've got this." And I had no choice but to trust and to believe.

Confronting the obvious, finally, I started cycling through next steps in my head. I hadn't done obstetrics in years, but the algorithm ended at only one place.

"Are you going to take her uterus?" I asked Dr. Kavi.

"We're not there yet, but we might get there," he responded, looking me in the eye.

"What about interventional radiology?"

He looked away. "Too many sources of bleeding to embolize all, and too long to get the team called in and set up. We're going to try a couple more uterine compression stitches and a balloon, and I've got a colleague scrubbing in to help."

Eventually, perhaps mercifully, the nurses took the babies.

Dr. Maties decided it was time to intubate Lindsey and put her under general anesthesia, and it was time for me to get out of that room.

If I had felt no sense of control inside the OR, the place where normally I control everything, I felt even less in control outside the room. Not that I had anywhere to be—except I was now a father, and maybe a soon-to-be solo father at that. At that point I didn't know where the babies had gone; I didn't know where my mother-in-law had gone; I didn't know if, when, or where Lindsey would turn up; and I was powerless to do anything but wander around. That in itself was more difficult than I might have thought. I later learned that children's hospitals are deliberately laid out in a confusing manner, with no straight hallways toward windows, no exit signs, and lots of ungridded hallways, the idea being if someone tries to make off with a baby, they'll get confused and not be able to get out before security can nab them. Everything was beige and anonymous, every hallway looked like every other hallway, every turn looked like every other turn; I had no idea where I was. Lost in a maze of beige, with no way to locate myself and no way to find my way out.

CHAPTER 2

THIS HOUSE IS NOT A HOME

THERE SHE LAY, eyes closed, body still, beneath crisp sheets of white, just a few hours after she had bled nearly to death, saved only by the quick, decisive, and skilled minds and hands of her surgeon and anesthesiologist. As I stood there in the ICU, a guest in a place where I usually feel at home, I looked down at her, knowing she would be crushed to learn she could not carry more children after this, but relieved, I hoped, as I was, because this had been the only way to save her life, her body ravaged by all she'd endured. The night in the ICU had seemed endless, with Lindsey hooked up to a ventilator, "sleep" forced on her with drugs, and more blood products dripping into her veins to keep her stable overnight. To look at her now, in this state of peace, of repose, you'd never have guessed all that had happened; it might have all been a dream and she was asleep at home, if not for the breathing tube wedged between her lips. Her struggle hadn't ended when she left the OR for the ICU; she stayed intubated, the ventilator necessary to breathe for her, given the risk of lung damage from the twenty or so units of blood she'd needed, and kept needing, to keep her blood counts up, to keep her blood pressure up. The whole night I had been downstairs, fighting sleep, in the hospital bed meant for Lindsey, Ayn asleep on the couch under the window, waiting for news of the next lab test result to offer hope of improvement. But each result, each follow-up, brought only partial relief. Maybe the blood count had gone up, but not as much as we'd hoped. Maybe the CT scan didn't show an obvious source of bleeding, but neither was it totally normal, and—*wait, is that something there?* We couldn't tell; we'd just have to watch and wait and see what happened. When I opened my eyes, the beige world of the hospital took on a blue-gray tone in the dark. I could faintly make out the difference between the wall and the window, dark as it was in the middle of the night. The moon was out there somewhere, giving off just the faintest shade of light behind the clouds, or what I would later realize was smoke from nearby wildfires, whose reach would soon take on the proportions of an apocalypse. I was there in the dark, afraid, exhausted, and alone. But I wasn't alone, not really; in the nursery were Baby A and Baby B, healthy and happy, nearly six and a half pounds each, and oblivious to the drama that had surrounded their birth, to the agony that had surrounded their conception, and, with any luck, to all that would follow in the next few months.

Lindsey did come off the ventilator that morning, though, a sign that she was safe and stable enough to breathe on her own, that she would likely survive. Her big brown eyes finally opened, and they darted around the room rapidly, taking it all in almost like a skittish fawn. Then she whipped her gaze back to me, staring at me directly. Her voice was hoarse and scratchy, her tone soft and sweet, like a tired child on the cusp of her own dreams. She said, "I died."

Against the backdrop of the beeps and clicks and pumps and monitors, I could barely make out what she said. It's not that I didn't hear her, or didn't understand; rather, I didn't believe her. I had been there, in that room, with her. And I have known death. I have seen it and touched it and caused it. I have marveled in its finality, its silence, its oppressive, final stillness. I have seen with my own eyes and felt with my own hands more times than I can count that shift, that moment when the lights go out, when the color changes from pink to gray, when that uniquely human warmth turns to shivers of ice. Gone are all the little things the body does to let us know it's alive: the warmth, the chest rising and falling, the sounds made by the heart and the gut, the urine streaming down the Foley catheter drip by precious golden drip. Gone, too, are all those beeps and buzzes that our monitors make to show us a proxy for life. It isn't until you come face-to-face with a dead person that you fully appreciate all it is that makes us alive.

In my lifetime as an anesthesiologist and intensive care physician, I have had more than a casual relationship with death. My contact is visceral, hands-on. I don't write orders to be followed; I touch, and do, and see, and feel. I pound chests; I stick necks with giant needles for organ and dialysis support, piercing skin, fat, and vein; I tube throats. I see the fear in people's eyes; I hear their last agonal; I feel their clammy, sweaty skin; I smell their breath, that sour, sticky breath of the sick, of decay, of death. I pull their dislodged dentures out of their mouths with a gloved hand, bits of their last meal still caked on. I can tell when they're getting just enough circulation from the CPR to begin to fight our attempts to breathe for them, that most primitive of brain-stem functions, the struggle to breathe, breaking through. I can feel their sweat, their sticky, glistening, pasty sweat, as my gloved hand slides off their jaw every time I try to squeeze life into their lungs. I can hear the snapping and crackling and popping of rib joints as they fail under the crushing weight of chest compressions, meant to push enough blood to the brain to prevent catastrophic, permanent brain injury. The cost of doing business, we say, but the deal almost never goes through, and I frequently find myself the deliverer of anguish to those who remain, the loved ones who, hoping for the best, wanted "everything done," either in denial or out of love or fear, until they hear from me that everything *was* done, that everything we did was simultaneously too much and not anywhere near enough. That the sweat they see on my brow is from the very real, very physical, very dirty and visceral relationship with their loved one's death. Or, what's worse, that we were kind of successful, that all the force we brought to bear kind of worked, and the body is technically alive, technically making the noises, technically twitching and moving, sort of, but the brain is mush and even though sometimes the patient moves his head when you walk into the room, he's not coming back. This is the most complicated part of my job, when I am balancing what I *think* I know to be true as a doctor—the physical truths of the body, health, physiology—with the weight of the emotional story of a patient's entire life, the web of relationships, their faith, their career, their unmet hopes, their unrealized dreams. It all sits with us in this room, with a weight and measure equal to the reality of their ailing body.

So when Lindsey told me she had died, I didn't believe her, because I'd been there, and because I know what I know, I've done what I've done, and I've seen the ugliness I've seen. It must have been a dream. And yet the night before, when they'd shuttled me out of the operating room so they could put her to sleep and intubate her, she was nearly bleeding to death. All told, they had already transfused twenty units of blood in her; in my lifetime, I have seen that amount of blood transfused maybe a couple of dozen times and maybe, *maybe,* half of those patients had survived. People say all the time, "Oh, I almost died," but I know what "almost dying" looks like, and Lindsey had been it. Seeing the blood on the floor, the sweat on her brow, and the gray of her skin, I'd known when I left her that there was a very real chance she might not make it. Could her heart have stopped? Could her blood pressure have been low enough that her brain wasn't getting enough oxygen? Maybe something *had* happened. Maybe she *had* died, at least a little.

Lindsey and I spent more than five miserable years, the first years of our marriage, trying to get pregnant, something so isolating and lonely and terrible that the word *terrible* doesn't fully capture it. Four egg retrievals, four embryo transfers, freezing, thawing, genetic testing, each an opportunity to be disappointed. Each cycle, a barrage of medications to inject into her swollen skin, the fear that any missed dose, any aberrant shot, would ruin the whole cycle, followed by the inevitable disappointment of failure, the uncertainty of the cause, and the blame and recrimination directed at our fertility doctor, or at medicine in general, or at me, for not doing more, not knowing more, not protecting her from these disappointments. Just writing these words now, years later, strikes me cold with a kind of indignation; I thought, at least at the time, that I had done the best I could, and yet she was so angry with me when each cycle failed. But if I'm honest with myself, it's probably more accurate to say that *she* spent more than five years trying to get pregnant, and I spent those same years just sort of in a fog of ambivalence, simultaneously trying to help shepherd us through the medical world of fertility care and then defending "medicine" when none of it worked. When I ask her about it now, she simply says that she was upset with me because when things got difficult I checked out, a knee-jerk reaction that I now realize I learned at a very young age in order to survive. She didn't care much for the explanations; she just wanted it to work. But it didn't, or wouldn't, or couldn't, or might eventually, but who knew. At various points there was talk of adoption, exploration of surrogates, and we went so far as to interview agencies and individuals. All of these difficult, sad, expensive, and heart-wrenching things, without even knowing for sure if I wanted kids at all. And then one day it *did* work, sort of.

When I went into medicine, part of the appeal was the perception that it was concrete. If the test was positive, you had the disease, or whatever, and that was that; you could get on with the business of curing it. The ongoing realization of just how untrue this is has been a humbling journey, but never more so than in the specialized field of fertility care. When you see those commercials for home pregnancy tests on TV, you think the results are very binary: either the blue line shows up and you're pregnant, or it doesn't and you're not. In contrast, after a cycle of IVF and embryo insertion, when it's time for a pregnancy test to see if it worked, you go to a lab and they draw blood and you get an actual number for the hormone level. You're supposed to go exactly ten days after the embryo is implanted and the number is supposed to be above 100. Every time prior for us, the number had been zero. On our fifth cycle, we ended up going in early, on day nine, and the number was 78. Not 100, but not yet at day ten, either. There we were, standing next to the car, outside the Thursday farmers' market near the Marin Civic Center, on the phone with our fertility doctor struggling to place ourselves on the most definitive binary in the human condition: Were we pregnant or not?

"Let's just go back to the lab for a retest in a few days and see."

"But are we pregnant?"

"We have to wait for the next one to know anything."

"But it's not zero; it's never been not-zero before. Surely we're pregnant?"

"Let's do another hormone level in a couple of days. . . ."

Pretty soon we did another test, and that showed a result higher than they wanted, so nobody knew what the hell was going on. Maybe it was a normal variation; maybe it was a giant multiplying tumor with fatal implications. Only in medicine, only in the endeavor that most terrifies us because it involves life and death, could something be equally likely to be great or horrific, with no way to tell other than to just wait.

"Or," they also said, "maybe it's twins."

At the first ultrasound, the physician was excited to show

us our, what, fetus? Embryo? Zygote? Baby? Just a little dark round spot in a field of speckled white, like the snow on an old TV. We cried, probably, or Lindsey did, and we could finally take a breath and be happy that, if just for a minute, or a day, or a week, there was something to feel other than sadness and loss and fear.

"Say, what's that other little dark spot? The small, sort of wonky-looking one at the bottom there?"

What I remember them answering went like this: "Oh, that. That's probably just a little ditzle or a partially formed whatever. You put in two embryos, right? That's just the second one, but you can see how it's not developed at all; those just resorb over time." And with that answer firmly received and processed as true, I walked out of that room thinking we were having a baby; I learned years later that everyone else in that room heard an entirely different answer and walked out thinking we were having twins.

But nine months later in the ICU, her tone low and hoarse from the irritation of the breathing tube that had just been removed, Lindsey said again, "I died," and then she recounted for me the most fantastical and detailed version of the go-to-the-light story I'd ever heard. She was staring off into the distance as she talked about hovering over the operating room and then being drawn into the most magnificent, glorious, intoxicating light. And there, in this vibrant, soothing, reassuring light, she saw her dad. There was a haze at first, then a crispness, a bright vibrancy, like the magic button that takes an iPhone photo from mediocre to brilliant. He was standing there, but not alone; behind him were ancestors, dozens of them, and she had had the distinct impression they had been waiting. Behind him she had been able to see each person and recognize them by their face, and she listed them by name for me there in the ICU. They stood on a huge football field, floating in a sky of pale blue, all dressed in suits, khakis, or cotton dresses, like in the painting *American Gothic,* as if for church . . . or a funeral. Everyone there looked healthy; not young, but healthy, as if the jump to heaven had revitalized them. All in line, and all looking at her, telling her, pleading with her—not with voices but with their faces, with the energy of their spirit, of sadness—to go back. *Go back! It isn't your time.* And it wasn't; as she drifted back to sleep, I could feel her breath, feel her tan-pink skin radiating warmth and life.

The medical explanation for visions like this is "anesthesia, sedating medications, maybe some cerebral hypoperfusion, yada, yada, yada," but that's just hand-waving. We simply don't know, and probably could never know, what happens in our brains and souls at that moment when the body is too sick to support life. For Lindsey, it was something greater than what the medical facts or jargon could describe. It was something as real as my standing there in the ICU room. Had it been a dream? A spiritual awakening? Did it mean something? Did it lay out or reinforce her destiny to stay alive to mother these children? To do something else? I knew she had never *actually* "died," in the strict, medical binary between alive and dead as I knew it, so precise and clinical. But I also knew that for far too long her blood pressure had been far too low to be safe, as she bled and bled and bled, her body giving everything it had in service of these new lives, the ones she wanted so badly. These lives. Three new lives. The twins', obviously, but also hers as a mother—as something more, I guess, than what she had with me. And, I guess, over time, maybe a fourth. Maybe mine.

When Lindsey and I talk about this now, with a few years of distance from the intensity of it, she remembers drifting in and out of consciousness on the OR table, holding her hand up above her head, like a child holding a balloon, while her anesthesiologist, Dr. Maties, held her hand during it all, telling her to hold on, that she wasn't letting go of her. Lindsey was certain that during this dream, this near-death experience, as her family was *pushing* her from that in-between world back to this one, that there was another voice, another force, this one *pulling* her back to us. That force came from Dr. Maties's hand, from the very real physical connection, the hand-to-hand, doctor-to-patient, soul-to-soul connection she was creating during that most precious and tenuous moment between life and death. Real or not, a more beautiful and perfect thing I cannot conjure.

CHAPTER 3

FROM THE ASHES: MORE ASHES

WHETHER BY DESIGN or not, accountability for my babies came on gradually. In the hospital, particularly while Lindsey was still in the ICU, the girls had their own nurse, a nursery where they were kept, and lactation specialists and other nurses who shuttled them between and betwixt their various stations without much input or effort from me. Could the girls tell? Could they tell I didn't know what I was doing, and maybe didn't want to know, or at least didn't know how to want to know? Did the medical staff do this out of pity, knowing I had to look after my wife, who had nearly died, or was this just how it worked? The full troupe, babies and all, arrived in the ICU around ten that first morning, minutes after Lindsey was taken off the ventilator that had breathed for her overnight, minutes into her recounting her visions of death from the night before. This was the first feeding visit of many, because, as they kept saying, if she didn't start right then, her milk supply would never catch up. "There are two of them, after all," people repeated, as if I could somehow forget. And so there they were: nurse, lactation specialist, two babies, and their mother, on the front end of a physical and emotional recovery that would take months if not years, even though we didn't yet know it.

Every three hours, night or day, the whole crew would march up to the fourth-floor ICU for a feeding session. I have pictures of that first time, Lindsey in the ICU, connected to what would seem to many like a million wires and tubes but which to me were invisible, just business. Connected also to two newborns, who were also in many ways invisible to me. Her smile was big, genuine, but in retrospect delirious and confused; she told me later that looking at that picture was like looking at a stranger. She didn't remember any of that moment. I felt so grateful that we had around-the-clock care and help with everything, including breastfeeding. That team was extraordinary, and when Lindsey confessed quietly on the second or third morning that she would often forget why she was in the hospital or that she even had babies, they wrote a new message on the dry-erase board by her bed each morning to remind her. The notes would say things like "Good morning, Lindsey! You have two very healthy baby girls that cannot wait to see you today!" Meanwhile, countless lights and beeps and clicks and waveforms and numbers were talking to me, speaking my language, crowding out everything else, telling me whether she was okay or how not-okay she might be.

I remember the first *real* time I walked into an ICU. Not like the times as a visitor, checking in on my grandpa after one of his multiple heart surgeries at the Mayo Clinic in Minnesota; not even like the times as a medical student on rotation in the ICU, where you're just expected not to break anything. The first time I was burdened by the yoke of accountability, of expectation, was something else entirely. I had finished medical school and was in my internship year at the University of Chicago Medical Center. It was the first day of my monthlong rotation in the ICU, and I was waiting in the conference room at five thirty in the morning to take over from the previous intern, who was clocking out at the end of her own monthlong rotation. Eventually she came in, frenetic with everything that was in front of her. She'd been working for twenty-four hours straight. That it was the very last hour of her very last shift there didn't even seem to enter her consciousness. She was all business, her red hair tied up in a bun and her green scrub pants tied loosely around her waist. She sat down and got right to it with her "sign-out," in which she went over all of the patients she had been responsible for. One patient stuck out to me:

> Ms. Jones, bed 8, 55 yo African-American Female with breast cancer, mets to chest well, lungs, and

> brain. Transferred from SNF with altered mental status, probably from a UTI, which led to sepsis and septic shock, now on the ventilator, pressors, and with renal failure and impending need for continuous hemodialysis. Family has changed status to "comfort care." When the family is all here, extubate the patient, start a morphine drip and titrate to comfort.

What this translates to is that the patient was a fifty-five-year-old African American woman who should have been in her prime but had been struck with breast cancer that had spread not just locally, to her chest wall, but to her lungs and brain as well, meaning there was no chance of cure. She'd been sick enough to have been at a skilled nursing facility, essentially a nursing home; there she'd developed a urinary tract infection, which is common in sick older folks who spend most of their time in bed, and she'd become delirious, which prompted the staff there to send her to the hospital. Because her infection had worsened and developed into septic shock, she'd come to the ICU for life support, including a mechanical ventilator to help her breathe and continuous infusions of medications to artificially raise her blood pressure to a safe level. Even with all that support, her kidneys had shut down, forcing the family to grapple with the prospect of starting dialysis, which requires a painful, invasive procedure to insert a very large plastic tube into the veins of her neck, just to prolong her life without any meaningful chance of her returning to health because her cancer was progressing so rapidly. Instead, and with the guidance of the doctors who'd been caring for her before I started my month in the ICU and "inherited" her, she would be transitioned to comfort care, meaning that all of the various life support machines and treatments would be stopped, painful things in her body such as breathing tubes would be removed, and she would be given medication to eliminate pain and the sensation of shortness of breath. What is sort of implied, but rarely said out loud, is that we will do all of this as we let the patient die.

As I sat in the room with that dying patient and witnessed family file in from all over the country in suits and dresses, it was not unlike the preparation for a birth, though in this case there was about to be one less person in the room. The energy in the room shifted; there was anticipation, nervousness. The family prayed, sang, read from the Bible. There was love and honor. They made me feel like one of them, even though I was white, I wasn't religious, and I couldn't carry a tune. All the monitors were turned off, and her breathing became imperceptibly irregular and she delicately touched her heart, almost as if she knew it was beating its last moments of life. Shortly thereafter I knew she had passed. In that moment I knew, even as an intern, that I wanted to hold this space for people like her, that I wanted to be an intensive care physician. I knew that not everyone would have family like this patient did, or even a single loved one by their side, but they would have me. My own heart had the capacity and purpose to make sure that each patient would be watched over with intentionality and peace as they exited this world.

I learned in my training how to control as much as I could in patients, using my knowledge and skill and the most aggressive treatments medicine had to offer, even those that caused pain or suffering, but in service of trying anything to make the patient stable, to make them better. And then, beyond that, with those limits reached and chaos reigning, I learned how to control the feelings of chaos within myself. But that first morning in the ICU with Lindsey, when I couldn't control what was happening around me, I relied on the lights and beeps to show me she was alive, the facts represented by those numbers helping to tamp down the chaos within me. Unlike my older patients in the ICU at the end of life, enduring difficult, frightening, or painful things without any real hope of improvement or even survival, what Lindsey endured was meant to return her to a full, beautiful life. From the transfusions to the lifesaving but life-altering hysterectomy, the one that meant she'd never birth another child, all of the treatments she underwent were difficult, painful, and frightening, but they were worth it for the chance of recovery. It didn't end there, though; there's always more to endure. Like the fact that they drew blood again while the babies were latching. At ten in the morning. Just like the night before, in the OR, my brain stem tingled.

They would've already drawn blood for morning labs around six, so there must have been something up, something they were following. Something they were worried about.

After the girls were done nursing, they'd get loaded up into a special baby cart to be wheeled back downstairs, while the lactation consultant would hook Lindsey up to a breast pump in order to stimulate her body to kick-start the hormonal cascade that gets the colostrum and later the breast milk flowing. In those early hours and days, she'd make just little dribbles of colostrum that they'd have me race down to the nursery to rub inside the girls' cheeks with a swab, to begin to populate their microbiome, the complex and increasingly essential population of bacteria in their bowels. Like having me cut the umbilical cords, or the proverbial instruction to "boil water," this started to have the feeling of make-work, something to keep me busy and engaged, as if I were actually helping. To be honest, though, that felt like about as much as I could do at the time to nurture them.

When those ten o'clock labs came back, Lindsey's blood counts were a little low. "Not dangerous, but lower than expected, given all the blood she's had so far," we were told. "We'll check again in a few hours and see where the trend is going." But I knew where the trend was going, and the follow-up labs and eventual CT scan confirmed it: As if the last twelve hours hadn't been horrific enough, it looked like Lindsey was still bleeding, internally this time, into her abdomen. The anxiety this created was intense. All those mechanisms to control fear seem useless when it's personal. I started to think about Lindsey becoming what we call an "ICU patient," one who develops a series of complications, and each attempt to fix one of those complications generates more problems. Though with Lindsey, we were hopeful that maybe her internal bleeding could be fixed through an interventional radiology (IR) procedure instead of a big open surgery. Interventional radiology is a huge success story fed by creativity, innovation, and, yes a profit motive. It is the specialty of using imaging technology, such as real-time X-ray, CT, and ultrasound, to guide tiny instruments into people's bodies to diagnose or treat—things like tubes to drain infected tissue, hemodialysis catheters to facilitate emergency treatment, tissue biopsy instruments to help make complex diagnoses, tubes and wires inside blood vessels to figure out where someone is bleeding and inject what amounts to superglue into those vessels to stop the bleeding from within. When IR works, it's like magic, sparing patients from much more dangerous and painful surgeries that carry a high risk of death. I knew, however, that Lindsey's CT scan didn't show a clear source of bleeding. When that's the situation, sometimes the IR physician has to embolize, or superglue, a larger number of vessels in a given area; if the tissue in that area doesn't have a good source of blood supply from other blood vessels, that tissue can die off and become an abscess, a pocket of infection. Then *that* needs to be addressed, and on and on. I've seen it all too often:

Something routine becomes complicated, and the complicated becomes a cascade of unexpected consequences, each of which can be dealt with, but only with an ever more imperfect and risky set of tools. It was the possibility of this cycle that spun in my head as Lindsey was wheeled away to the IR suite. It led to the terrifying, paralyzing thought that Lindsey might not completely recover. I wondered aloud whether I could parent the twins alone—and, silently, whether I *would* do it alone; if Lindsey did die, would I even keep them? Lindsey's mother, Ayn, who had been in the hospital with us all that time, scoffed at the worry I spoke out loud—of course I could do it, she told me. But that didn't address the worry I'd kept silent. Had I even wanted children in the first place? Who could tell now, amid all this angst and confusion?

But I didn't yet need to confront those first awful whisperings in my brain. The IR physician saw a place to embolize, the images looked good, and Lindsey's blood counts stabilized. She was even able to leave the ICU a day or so later (although I think she'd gotten used to all the attention; for part of the time she'd been the only patient in the whole unit, and of course everyone loved it when the twins showed up for their feedings). Those first few days out of the ICU, though, she was racked with pain from her surgeries and could barely walk. Getting up to go to the bathroom, for instance, was a painful affair that required at least one helper and had to be carefully orchestrated.

I have a picture somewhere, deep in my phone, of the "name board" we had created on our hospital dry-erase board, the one usually reserved for patient data. When Lindsey wasn't wincing from pain, or being endlessly monitored and tested for everything from internal bleeding to wound infections, and when we weren't learning how to nurse not one but two babies who were a combined thirteen pounds, we'd glance at that dry-erase board and then slink away, overwhelmed and intimidated by it all.

I'm not sure how cognizant Lindsey even was during this time as we tossed around names we liked: Lucia, Giulia, Sydney, Alessandra, Caroline, and more. Although we knew we were having two babies, the one combination for which we hadn't planned was two girls. As we stared at the dry-erase board day after day, I was reminded of the story my mother tells of my own naming, which dragged on and on, even after leaving the hospital. My father—impatient, I'm sure, given what I know about him—blurted out, "Just name the damn thing George!" and so here I am, Christopher George.

In a dance that I've subsequently learned is a bit of a cliché, the nurses and medical staff insist there is no rush to settle on names, that you can decide later, while the paperwork person insists, with ever more fervor each day, that taking a long time to decide is the first of many inevitable derelictions of our duty as parents. Little did I know at the time how inconsequential this first failure was compared to all I would encounter once we went home and the real work of parenting started.

Eventually, though, Baby A (the ditzle, the partially formed whatever, who initially I didn't think was real on that first ultrasound) became Olympia Frances, or simply Pia; Olympia to honor my Greek heritage and Frances to honor my Greek grandmother, Fran, and Lindsey's grandfather Frank. Baby B, the one who saved Lindsey's life by swimming around so vigorously and being so unmonitorable that we ended up in the operating room—the only place a patient with that much bleeding has any hope of surviving—became Elisabetta in Italian, a nod to Lindsey's heritage, and Elizabeth in English, or Isa as we've come to affectionately call her. Elizabeth is Lindsey's sister's middle name and also the name of her family's matriarch, her great-grandmother, Elizabeth Williams, affectionately known as Bess.

We did ultimately settle into a kind of routine for several days in the hospital, after Lindsey was well enough to leave the ICU. The girls would spend the night in the nursery, attended to by a cadre of nurses, sipping donated breast milk until Lindsey's own supply caught up, allowing us some rest. Then, during the days, it was visits from the obstetrics team, guilting us for staying as long as we had; from the pediatrics team, with their bright smiles and encouragement about the girls' weights; from the nurses, bringing in babies to be fed; from the lactation consultants, helping us with the breast pump; and from the physical therapists, trying to train Lindsey on how to walk up the stairs she'd encounter at home. Even the anesthesia team came by a few times a day, mostly residents whom I'd helped train over the prior couple of years, to pay social calls and see the twins. With all that help and guidance, it almost seemed like babies could be manageable, and in any case, it was just simple tasks at this point—feed, burp, change, wipe, swaddle, and then rinse and repeat, without the eventual crushing weight of real accountability, being surrounded by help of every kind.

After five or six days, though, the room was starting to smell like the salami that I'd been storing in our Yeti cooler, we'd exhausted the best of the hospital's food menu, and we'd long since run out of the produce we'd brought from home nearly a week prior. I wouldn't exactly say we were itching to leave, or even ready, but we both kind of knew it was time. I'd begun to pack up our things—the Yeti with the food; all the free diapers, wipes, towels, and bottle supplies the hospital gives out (and charges the insurance company for); and, finally, the girls. I placed them into their infant car seats, the ones I'd bought months prior and memorized all the straps and clips for. I'd even had to watch a YouTube video to get it right. As I carefully adjusted each nylon webbing strap against their tiny, compliant, blanketed bodies, I remember thinking how this was the first of the uncountable times they'd be buckled into some kind of car seat until they were practically teenagers, and how different that seemed compared to when my older brother and I had been kids, sloshing around the backseat of cars with mere lap belts to hold us in place on upholstery that showed a number of cigarette burns. I thought, too, about my brother, who years before had brought his own daughter home from the hospital. Had he been happy? Proud? Joyful? Or had he felt the way I did, simultaneously checked out and terrified?

CHAPTER 4

GREW UP TALL; DIDN'T GROW UP STRAIGHT

UNLIKE THE WAY my daughters' birth unfolded, no one heralded my entrance into this world. My brother at least can claim the family story of nearly being birthed on the back of a snowmobile racing toward the hospital in Windom, Minnesota, a small rural city in the Coteau des Prairies, a plateau in the southwestern part of the state. This makes it sound quaint, but I saw that place later in life, and my memory is of a godforsaken bluff at the edge of a godforsaken prairie, a nothing-burg surrounded by nothing. It was during the blizzard of 1974, and the snow was so deep and the area so remote that the roads were impassable to cars. Back then, the cars were all rear-wheel drive and tire chains were *actual* chains; all-wheel drive and SUVs were still at least fifteen years away. Our parents had no money, and so I can't conjure how they had access to a snowmobile, something that mostly the well-off had back then, but one way or another it happened. They made it to the hospital in time, but the story remains part of our family lore, trotted out from time to time to say how different, how hard life was back then. In contrast, I was born, barely fourteen months later, in an anonymous hospital in an anonymous suburb outside of Minneapolis.

My mom found out that she was pregnant with my older brother the last month of her senior year of college. She had started dating my dad less than a year earlier. They had a shotgun wedding when she was two or three months pregnant in her hometown Lutheran church, and then my dad's Greek family insisted that they get married all over again, this time when she was six months pregnant, in the Greek Orthodox church. My mom said she could literally hear the attendees snickering at how much she was showing as her dad walked her down the aisle for a second time. When my brother was three months old, my mom was hospitalized for pleurisy and pericarditis (inflammation and fluid collection in the sacs surrounding the lungs and heart, respectively), and that's when she found out she was pregnant with me. With both my brother and then me, she went back to work after four weeks of time off (all of it unpaid) after giving birth; she would drop us off at an in-home daycare in the dark before sunrise and pick us up in the dark after sunset. At one point her employer instituted mandatory overtime, which meant she would have to start working six days a week, but she thought to ask her doctor to write her a note that qualified her for disability, so she wouldn't have to work Monday through Friday and then every Saturday, too. Some of her female colleagues, even some with kids, didn't want to lose their jobs because of what they saw as a risky exemption, so they worked that sixth day as well.

It shouldn't have been this hard for my mom, Diane. She is a bright and motivated woman, and I'm sure I got my own aptitude for learning from her. Neither her parents nor any of her siblings went to college. She herself didn't even think of going to college until her junior year of high school. She grew up in southern Minnesota, in a rural town called Owatonna that is mostly surrounded by farmland. Her family didn't get indoor plumbing until 1958. Her dad's family were carpenters, building barns and fences for the farmers in Owatonna and the surrounding area. Her mom's family were farmers, homesteaders from Denmark. People mostly farmed beets, wheat, and soybeans in this part of the country. However, my grandmother worked as a secretary for an insurance company all throughout my mom's childhood; she was the only mother my mom knew who worked outside the home in Owatonna. My mom took care of her two younger siblings her entire life, feeding them, dressing them for school, picking them up after school, and watching them until dinnertime. She doesn't remember playing or having friends in her childhood or even thinking much about her future. In her junior year of high school, my mom had a history teacher, Miss Hart, a self-described spinster who would mutter under her breath during class that there was no reason to get married or have a family, which was radical and even scandalous in 1960s rural Minnesota. It's funny to think that during this same time, Lindsey's mom was taking African American history classes in high school in San Francisco, marching for peace against the Vietnam War, and burning bras. Anyway, Miss Hart was a notoriously difficult teacher. In fact, my mom's father had dropped out of high school at fourteen to avoid being in Miss Hart's class. But my mom loved Miss Hart and pushed herself to get in the teacher's good graces. In her senior year Mom had an English teacher, Mr. Bennett, who pulled her aside after school to give her some pointers so that she would be "properly prepared for college." When she said she wasn't going to go to college, he looked shocked and told her she should really reconsider this. Mr. Bennett shouldn't have been surprised that my mom didn't have plans to go to college; she can't recall any other women in her graduating class going to college. She went home that night after talking to Mr. Bennett and asked her parents whether, if she worked for a year after graduating from high school and saved money, they would give her their blessing to attend college. But they were noncommittal.

Still, something drove her, as the summer after graduating from high school she worked at Federated Insurance as a keypunch operator to save up money, and then went to Mankato

State University, sight unseen, that fall. She hated her first year because it all just felt too alien—until she discovered the college radio station and made lifelong friends. The university was where she would eventually meet and then start dating my dad her senior year. My dad, Nick, was older than my mom but never actually graduated from college. Both his parents were Greek immigrants, and he was the eldest of four boys. He grew up in St. Louis Park, Minnesota, where his parents ran a dry-cleaning shop. Once they married, my mom essentially supported all four of us by working at Blue Cross Blue Shield; my dad was always driving, first for Yellow Cab, and later doing long-haul charter bus routes all across the country. We lived in Brooklyn Park, a suburb of Minneapolis, in a two-bedroom apartment, and during this whole time we had only one car, so my mom would often walk miles to and from the bus to work and childcare, pushing one infant in a stroller and pregnant with another, until finally a female colleague offered to sell Mom her mother's barely used car for a thousand dollars, saying that my mom needed this car more than anyone else she knew. Like many economically stressed families, we moved a lot the first few years of my life, so much that my mom said she felt like they were running from the law even though no one had committed any crimes. But I get it; when you are on the move like that, you are anxious, panicked, and generally afraid. My mom was the stable force within our family, and my dad had a wild, unpredictable temper that made it difficult to keep jobs, housing, and relationships. In 1977, when I was two years old, my mom went to work for Honeywell in operations, helping Honeywell employees get paid on insurance claims. She eventually worked at Honeywell for thirty-five years in various roles. At some point she started a master's program but eventually quit because of time constraints. At her retirement, someone at Honeywell noted that there were few other employees who had worked competently across so many departments. And yet in my family there never seemed to be enough money. The American dream this was not.

In 1980, my parents divorced; I was five and my brother was six. I remember neither hearing an explanation nor being surprised. My dad yelled a lot, and I can recall feeling nervous when I was in the house with him. When he moved out, we had to leave our duplex in Champlin, a rural suburb of Minneapolis. Even though 1980 doesn't seem that long ago, my mom had a hard time finding a landlord who was willing to rent an apartment to a single mother. Wayzata, where we ultimately settled, was a politically liberal place—and in the best school district in the state, which wound up defining who we became. As a child of divorce and without much money, though, I grew up feeling like I was on the outside looking in. I remember so clearly on the first day of kindergarten being on the classroom rug and overcome with the realization that except for me, everyone already knew everyone else. I hadn't gone to Peppermint Fence preschool, where all these kids had met and become friends. This was the first of many years in which I'd walk into a new classroom in September not knowing anyone, even though most people there knew at least someone, often many someones, because they'd all gone to the same few schools. Somehow I was already late to the party; the cliques had been formed, and I was different from these kids. One parent instead of two; an apartment instead of a house; jeans from Wrangler instead of Guess; not sure what "Tahoe" or "Maui" were when classroom talk turned to family vacations or spring break. My father was still in the picture at this point, but eventually he would disappear entirely, making me feel even more alone and different. We stayed close to his family throughout this time, which in hindsight was a heroic act of selflessness on my mother's part. This is something I've always felt extraordinarily grateful to my mother for; I'm sure it couldn't have been easy being around Nick after the divorce, but she and the family made a real effort, and to this day my brother and I remain closer to our dad's family than to our mother's. Some of my clearest, happiest memories as a child were the raucous family Christmas Eve celebrations in my Greek grandparents' tiny house, bursting at the seams with screaming and laughing cousins, watched over by aunts and uncles eating spanakopita and moussaka and drinking ouzo. My grandmother was a terrible cook, but she and the others made good jokes, and people were happy around my Greek grandparents' table. I remember feeling free from my worries when I was there. I fit in.

By three, I had taught myself to read; shortly thereafter I invented my own language, and I recall being taken out of regular classes as early as third or fourth grade for testing and then being reassigned to new "high-potential" classes. I also remember being picked on for having long hair and the wrong clothes. Once in the middle of class a girl named Heidi looked me straight in the eye and sang "They called her H-I-P-P-Y" about me and my uncut hair. This was probably something that she'd never in a million years remember, but I, obviously, still do. I was mortified. In fourth grade, there was a creative writing class that only a few of us were asked to participate in, and it was the only time in school that I can recall feeling comfortable. We were taught how to write a "novel," and mine was a whodunit set in Scotland and involved the detective getting botulism, preventing him from solving the case, because I thought an unsolved case was more unexpected than a solved one and also left the door open for a sequel. Throughout this class, I just let my goofy thoughts and ideas fly. But in general I didn't have close, mentoring relationships with teachers; there was no one who believed in me or took me under their wing. Instead, I remember being sent to the hall with some regularity to be scolded, even into junior high. I know some of this was because I goofed off in class too much, unable to resist the few opportunities to connect with a classmate who finally wasn't picking on me. Aside from that, I felt like I was mostly on my own.

With time I have come to realize that the economic problems were just surface details in a childhood filled with discomfort and loneliness. "Feeling poor" is a convenient way to describe my isolation and fear, but the real issue in my upbringing wasn't as much economic as it was that my mother was sick and probably depressed for my entire childhood. Who could blame her? She had been fighting to succeed her whole life, first in a family that didn't support her and then with a husband who actively took her down. Most of my early memories were of her lying on the couch after work, often with a cold washcloth on her forehead and seemingly in pain. On the weekends she would go to her darkened bedroom and close the door. We had a pool in our apartment complex and I loved going, but she rarely took us. It was too much to go down the two flights of stairs and the short distance to the courtyard where the enclosed pool was located. Her job started at six thirty in the morning, leaving my brother and me to fend for ourselves before and after, starting in first grade. We would make our own breakfast and take ourselves to the bus stop, and starting at age eight we also did our own laundry and made dinner. I'm not sure what the alternative would've been; she had to go to work to pay the bills or we'd have been out on the street. These are things that I know now build character and made me self-reliant, but I was scared a lot as a kid. My mother's fears became mine. She would cry sometimes, unsure if she could continue to provide for us, or she would tell us how broke we were, how close to the line of collapse, so as to keep us from asking for too much. A child plagued by these worries misses something elemental, some freedom of thought that allows them to blossom. When you feel like your parent is barely holding on, you learn very early on not to turn to them for anything because the perceived balance between their own life and death and by extension your existence is so precarious that even the joys, never mind the troubles, will overwhelm them. The three of us lived together in a parallel existence, in universes so far apart from one another that I don't ever recall sharing my day with my mom, something that is such a basic, even clichéd part of childhood. I don't think my mom ever asked about my day, and I don't recall ever telling her. I kept everything inside.

My brother Steve and I shared a bedroom until I went away to college, but I wouldn't say we were close or shoulders for each other to lean on. We all coexisted, together but separately deep into our respective worlds. I recall listening to comedy on cassette tapes in my top bunk when I was in elementary school late at night, and Steve would listen in on his bottom bunk because I didn't have a headset yet. Eddie Murphy's *Delirious* and Sam Kinison's *Louder than Hell* were my favorites. I don't know how I even got these tapes—they were wildly inappropriate for a fourth grader—but I loved comedy and I loved laughing; maybe it made me feel like I did at those Greek family dinners. It feels like an odd thing to say, but laughing felt like an escape.

My brother and I were only fourteen months and one grade apart, but we almost never saw each other outside that shared bedroom because I was in those high-potential classes, which were on the other side of the elementary school campus. When we did see each other, we fought a lot. Maybe all brothers fight, but with us the kicking and punching lasted into junior high, an age far too old for it to be about things like sharing toys. We weren't fighting over friends or girls; we might've just been angry kids, lashing out with our bodies to express the unspoken things hurting our souls, given all that surrounded us. I punched him once, right in the face, and broke one of his front teeth. He'd already broken that tooth once, as a kid, sliding face-first down a playground slide, so I'd only re-broken a repaired tooth. That distinction was a key part of my defense during the inquisition from our mother, but it did little to smooth things over, given that it happened on Thanksgiving with family visiting. But I felt victorious in that moment that I had finally "won," because he was bigger and stronger than me. I don't think we ever fought again. Something shifted, and while I wouldn't say we became friends, exactly, our teen years were better.

He taught me to drive, taking us out together in the car

we'd eventually share, the one new car our mom had ever bought, a 1984 Ford Tempo in desert tan with the three-speed transaxle and the 2.3-liter in-line four-cylinder engine cranking out maybe 80 horsepower. We'd go out west of town, on rural backroads with no traffic, and he'd let me take over, just going a mile or two, practically in slow motion, to get the feel of it. God, I loved the feeling of driving from the very first day we went out: the sense of control, the taste of freedom, the potential speed. It was intoxicating. Later, it was Steve who introduced me to music. He was into Nirvana (*Bleach,* not *Nevermind*) and Soundgarden (before *Badmotorfinger*), as well as Midwestern roots rock like The Jayhawks and the Gear Daddies' Martin Zellar; he asked for the Wilco double album *Being There* for his birthday one year, before it had even been released. He'd play Martin Zellar for me on a little boom box on the floor of our shared room, and I was taken by Zellar's seemingly autobiographical melancholy, the rural Midwestern sadness of not quite getting it right. But maybe someday.

When I was twelve our dad remarried, and my brother and I, along with some of my uncles and our grandpa, were in the wedding party. I remember all of us getting dressed together in rented polyester tuxedos in the basement of the Greek Orthodox church in Saint Paul, the one my own parents had gotten married in almost fifteen years earlier. We practically lived in this church as children; I still remember the particular metallic taste of the water from the water fountain in the basement, and the way the circles of dancing Greeks looked, hands clasped, arms rising and falling to the loud music in the fellowship hall at weddings, at funerals, and on just regular Sundays. But there in that basement bathroom, as we figured out together how to attach our cummerbunds, everyone was kind of making fun of our dad and the tuxes he'd picked out, in particular the multi-colored pin-striped tuxedo pants, and for the groom a cane and top hat. "I wouldn't shovel shit in these pants," my grandpa said, in the rough, loose-phlegmed voice of the chronic cigarette smoker he was. I laughed along with everyone else, and it felt good to have this sense of camaraderie that was so often lacking in my day-to-day life. But when I think about it now, it was odd to laugh at my own father on his wedding day, and it was maybe odder still that his own father was making such an angry crack. Within a year, my dad and his new wife moved to Arizona, and though I didn't know it at the time, I'd never see him or hear from him again. Nothing happened, no argument or falling-out; he simply moved and stopped calling us or reaching out. Time passed, and that was that.

In high school, someone with grades like mine might have been steered toward Advanced Placement classes or toward considering prestigious universities after graduation. I'm sure there was a college counselor in my high school, someone to identify bright kids and make sure they didn't fall through the cracks, but I'd never met that person. I didn't know at the time that my grades made me *that* special. At the time, I was thinking about being a schoolteacher and considered going to the University of Wisconsin, Eau Claire, a small regional state university that I'd heard had a good education major and was affordable. But then sometime during my junior year a letter showed up in the mailbox at home telling me to come to school on an upcoming Saturday to take a test. I felt like these tests had been a regular part of my life all the way through elementary and junior high, so I assumed this one was the same. I didn't think much of it, beyond being annoyed that I had to pull some strings to get out of work as a stocker at the local supermarket, where my brother also worked. But when I arrived for the test, it was in a regular classroom filled with just the smart kids. I would learn later that the "test" was the Preliminary Scholastic Assessment Test, or PSAT. Within weeks of my taking it, our apartment mailbox began to overflow with large thick envelopes filled with brochures about colleges all over the United States. Some schools even sent VHS tapes. Later still, I would learn I was a National Merit semifinalist, which means I had scored in the top 1 percent of students in Minnesota. I guess there was some application I had to do and endorsements I had to get from teachers to be a finalist—95 percent of semifinalists go on to be finalists—but I had missed that part of the memo and never filled out those forms.

Even with all the national college attention, I never thought of leaving our little corner of the Midwest. In the end I went not to the University of Wisconsin, Eau Claire, but instead to

Gustavus Adolphus College, a small private liberal arts college named for a Swedish king from the 1600s, because the minute I walked onto campus, I felt an unfamiliar sense of peace and comfort, and that was enough for me.

College changed everything for me. I could be myself, or, better said, I could discover who I actually was away from the heaviness of my childhood which felt like weights bearing down on me. There were still rich kids and poor ones, but the differences somehow became less visible; nearly everyone had some kind of work-study job, and nearly everyone lived in the same kind of dorm room. The town of nine thousand was so small it wasn't like the rich kids went to better restaurants and drank better beer; we were all stuck with Godfather's Pizza, the Chinese restaurant where my friend Ted kept bouncing checks, and drinking Milwaukee's Best from a keg at parties in the same dingy and cigarette-smoke-filled basements. No one cared much where you were from or what your parents did for a living; for guys, more important was whether you had game with girls or could shotgun a beer the right way. There was a small Greek fraternity and sorority system there, and in a move that made no sense to anyone before or since, I joined a fraternity. There were parties, and girls, and beer, and the kind of hanging out and having funny things happen that I'd never had before. I had stopped listening to comedy cassettes by then, but I laughed so much in college that I felt free. If I needed to put a pin in the moment when I started to unconsciously lock the past away and transition into the adult I saw myself as before Lindsey and I had kids, this would be it. Guys I became friends with then are still my best friends to this day. These guys set the foundation for my adult life, and even as I am writing this now I have a huge smile across my face. I love them in a way I don't think I knew was possible for my entire life up until college.

College is where I learned table manners and which fork to use, and where I learned leadership as the president of the fraternity and sorority system and as a collegiate fellow mentoring a group of underclass students in the dorms. It's where I learned how to talk to girls, smoke cigarettes without coughing, and be cool or at least fit in. I chose to major in psychology and philosophy, thinking I'd apply to graduate school, get a PhD, and become a psychologist and college professor. Something about understanding human behavior intrigued me (probably because I was so far from understanding my own), and the way psychology researchers used large numbers of subjects and complicated statistical rules seemed to really fit how my brain worked and the things I liked thinking about. At the end of my senior year I received a letter inviting me to a dinner on a Tuesday night. The sheet of paper had some Greek letters on it and there was no cost to go, so I showed up. Turns out I was elected to Phi Beta Kappa, a national honor society "that honors students who have demonstrated a broad and deep commitment to the liberal arts and sciences, excelling in a wide range of subjects rather than just one." It's a bit funny because I took only one science class my whole time in college, introductory geology, which was colloquially referred to as "Rocks for Jocks" because it was allegedly the easiest of the science classes. The hilarity of this is compounded by the fact that I would ultimately become a physician having taken only that one science class in college.

I ended up choosing a PhD program in counseling psychology at Iowa State, where I also got a full academic ride. My first year in the program I had to take advanced courses in pharmacology, and I found this *so* fascinating that it made me wonder if I was in the right PhD program. I was actually wondering this out loud to a total stranger in the computer lab (because it was 1998, after all, and that was still how you checked your email) and this girl started asking me a number of probing questions. After carefully listening to my answers, she said, "It kind of sounds like you should be a doctor." Her dad was a physician, I would later find out, but at the time I had never considered becoming one. I didn't know any doctors, none of my friends' parents were doctors, and no one in my family was in any type of medicine or nursing. But I knew I needed to follow this thing tickling my brain, even though at the ripe old age of twenty-two I thought it was too late to shift career tracks, that I should just run out the clock, finish my doctorate, and stick with the plan. So I talked myself into adding pre-med courses to my graduate classes and thesis work. That I was starting to have problems in the counseling practice part of the psychology curriculum—my teachers were wondering why it seemed so hard for me to connect with my student-clients at the University counseling center where we trained—seemed irrelevant to me. The university had a pre-med counselor who thought I was crazy for taking so many classes, but I was intimidated for a different reason: All the undergraduate students in my first-year chemistry class had just finished their high school science courses, and I assumed that despite the age difference they would be leaps and bounds ahead of me. Waiting for the bus that night outside the student union, I paged through the chemistry textbook, which I had just purchased at the bookstore. *Crazy,* I thought; *I don't know any of this stuff.* Math? Geology didn't have math! There were a handful of times I thought about giving up before I even started, but once I did start, I felt like a fish in water. I absorbed the material quickly, and in a year I'd finished the entire pre-med curriculum while finishing my master's in psychology at the same time. I crushed the MCAT, the Medical College Admission Test.

During this time, my friends were progressing in their jobs, buying houses, meeting people, and getting married. Some even started families. I didn't feel that same pull, and I always had my progress as an excuse; I had relationships, but I never really thought about them leading to having a family. I'd reasoned, at least subconsciously, that it would hinder my professional development. I'd never be able to do as well in school and in training, I assumed, if I had a wife and kids to manage and support, never mind that plenty of classmates did it just fine. I was able to push down the fact that my personal life and relationships weren't progressing, weren't rich and deep and intimate, because I was putting energy into becoming a physician.

It's more accurate, though, to say that on some level I was trying to have those real relationships but just didn't know how. My only exposure to intimacy was my family and the worry I felt for my mom. I didn't want to have a girlfriend if I had to worry about her in the same way, holding my breath in anticipation that she, too, would end up lying on the couch with a cold washcloth on her head or hidden away in her darkened bedroom all weekend crying. I thought a relationship was just about having another person to look after, another mouth to feed; it never occurred to me that it could be additive, or even synergistic. That perspective is even more comical to me now because even though Lindsey has been more professionally successful than me at various points in her career, during the periods when she's taking time off or consulting and I am paying all or most of the bills, I love it. I look at our life and feel an immense sense of pride that I can provide for us. But the version of me in my twenties, the one running from bar to bar, was still running from my past, and still keeping at arm's length anyone giving any hint that I would feel the same sense of responsibility that had weighed on me my entire childhood.

My twenties and thirties were littered with false starts that, at the time, I thought were just life—half-painful, half-hilarious interludes on the bumbling path toward eventual relationship success, not realizing that this wasn't actually how most people did it. Instead of dates and courtship and meeting families and progress, there were hurt feelings and angry shouting. There were thrown shoes and glass objects, the inevitable end to a repeating cycle of yearning for closeness that, once achieved, led to me shutting down and closing off. Maybe a better way to put it is that as soon as a woman felt close enough to me to need something from me, I was triggered. I had learned from my upbringing not to rely on others, but I had also learned from watching my mother what the stress of having people rely on her did to her during those lean years of layoffs and economic worry, and I could not repeat that in my own life.

This played out in my last relationship before meeting Lindsey; in our final argument, this woman, who at one point I believed did love me, said I didn't deserve her, that I didn't deserve anyone, and that I wasn't meant to be among "the humans." She also said she almost felt sorry for me, because she sensed I didn't even know why she was ending things, that I couldn't even really grasp what she'd been asking for, what was missing, and that her point about me not mixing well with "the humans" was so core to how she experienced me.

In the aftermath, a close friend of mine from college, when

I asked her what she thought of that woman's comments, put it in the starkest terms in an email so piercing and on-target that I've kept it now for nearly fifteen years:

> I would say that you might make people feel like your personal experience is the very most important and the person you are dating is cool if they fit in, but if they don't then you're cool with your own life and don't really need them to fit in. And the kicker is that it is virtually impossible for someone to fit in with your life. Because it is so flagrantly and unapologetically yours . . . I didn't really understand the extent or depth of your self-centeredness until I experienced it. And please don't take that negatively, because you are who you are because you have been self-focused so I see very positive attributes in that attitude as well. However, it makes relationships tough.

I have reread this a number of times over the years, and it gives me a shiver each time. Even if I wasn't conscious of how self-centered I was during all those supposedly formative years of my twenties and thirties, others close to me were. The ideas in that email sank in as familiar not because I'd heard them before but because I knew it was true of me then. It cuts so close to the bone that I can't help but feel a certain amount of love and respect for the person who said it: Knowing someone so profoundly isn't easy, and saying hard things like this is also not easy. To be truly seen and understood, even in a way that's not so flattering, by another person feels unlike anything else in the human experience. On the other hand, though, the assessment, accurate though it might have been, felt, and feels, damning. Was I really this cold? And what changed that I was finally able to truly let someone in? I wouldn't be able to answer that for years.

In 2001, I started medical school at the University of Minnesota. There is a theme throughout my academic career: I only applied to schools in the Midwest and I accepted offers from schools where I got a full ride or a huge academic scholarship. Residency, the place where you go after you receive your medical degree to train in your specialty, was no different. I attended the University of Chicago. It wasn't until 2008, when I was applying for fellowship programs, that I considered leaving the Midwest. At this point, I had been in the medical school system long enough—four years for medical school and four years for anesthesia residency—that I had noticed that the best students came from a small handful of schools, and those schools were largely (but not entirely) on the East and West Coasts. Plus, I felt like I had grown up during these eight years, I had experienced the world vicariously by being exposed to a broader pool of students and professors, and I was in a place where I could take it all in. I no longer felt the heavy burden of my family's well-being.

Within each medical practice or specialty, there are many paths a doctor can take: private practice, academia, public-service medicine. I was fairly certain I was going to do academic medicine, and within that I was looking at mission-driven medicine, focusing on the people who needed the care the most, no matter whether they could pay or not. Why did I choose anesthesiology over being a surgeon? I was in the top 5 percent of my medical school class and could have easily gone in that direction, yet I didn't ever truly consider being a surgeon because I couldn't handle that kind of longer-term relationship with my patients. I wouldn't say surgeons have long-term relationships with patients per se, but once you operate on someone, there is an enormous amount of dependency. Specialties like oncology, psychiatry, and primary care are defined by ongoing relationships with patients and the needs around them, and those were immediately off the table for me. At the time, I couldn't exactly explain why I didn't want that level of accountability nor those multi-year (or even multi-decade) relationships, but I would later understand that my ability to compartmentalize had its limits. Still, after my night with Ms. Jones and her family, I knew I had the capacity to care deeply, and that was why I chose to ultimately work in the ICU, as this allowed me to do meaningful one-on-one work with patients and their families over a comparatively short period of time, allowing me to get just a taste of that connection I'd been avoiding.

This was all looming in the back of my head as I was deciding between Stanford and UCSF for my fellowship—additional subspecialty training beyond residency. I had done enough training during my residency to become a board-certified anesthesiologist, but this extra training meant I could also get certified to practice intensive care medicine, caring for the sickest patients in the hospital, those on life support, with machines helping them live. I ultimately chose UCSF because I felt more comfortable there. It's a state school, and it resonated more with me; I felt more at home there. Like the University of Chicago, it was urban, it was slightly shabby, and, given that it oversaw the local county trauma center and veterans' hospital, a lot of underserved people received care there. Plus, in my specialty, there is no greater place to train than UCSF, and I'd come far enough in my own accomplishments and self-confidence, at least professionally, that I went for it, I got it, and I was proud to be there. Once I got to California, though, I felt like I had on that first day of kindergarten: as though everyone already knew one another, with me on the outside looking in. Physicians here came from the world's most prestigious universities, and many seemed to be familiar with one another already. I remember distinctly sitting in line at the security office, waiting to have my photo ID badge made, and watching people in line greet one another, presumably because they'd met at any of a small handful of other universities during past levels of training, during past lives. This felt different, though, compared to when I was younger; now I knew I was about to be part of that club.

California itself became like a dream for me: the ocean, the mountains, the wildlife, the sun, things I'd never expected to care about. In San Francisco, the air is always moving. It's not windy, but there is constant movement as the breeze and fog slide in from the ocean and the bay, swell up through the redwoods and into the rolling hills beyond. That natural movement doesn't produce a hectic, loud, or chaotic energy like you'd find in New York City, but it does create an energy; nothing sits still for long, and ideas and possibilities abound. And then there's the Sierra Nevada, the stunning line of mountains that runs the entire length of the state and encompasses such spectacular natural beauty as Lake Tahoe, Yosemite, and Mt. Whitney. The first time I flew over the range, my forehead pressed to the small oval glass window of the airplane, I understood why people trekked the Pacific Crest Trail, the 2,650-mile hiking route that runs from Mexico to Canada. To be immersed in these mountains suddenly seemed incredible, almost enviable. As we descended down into the Bay Area, I felt as though passing over this mountain range had delivered me to the *now* and, by extension, separated me from my past. Even though there wasn't someone I was trying to become, beyond the professional, or even something I was trying to unveil, that very physical mark of separation was liberating and powerful. Plus, these mountains made me feel hidden from view, separate from the rest of the country. I recall thinking almost immediately after arriving, *Oh, this is why people come here to be proudly gay, or to live in a commune, or to invent things that will change the world.* Not only were you were free to try new things, but you were encouraged to live outside the box. It was like I'd been waiting my entire life for someone to give me permission to be me, and I hadn't expected that permission to come in the form of geography. But here I was.

Fellowship training in intensive care had many of the same hallmarks as residency in anesthesia: hard work, long hours, and innumerable patient encounters that began to chip away at my reserve. Nonetheless, at the end of my year at UCSF, I was invited to stay on as faculty, which felt like a dream. If training at UCSF felt prestigious to me, working there felt like the ultimate stamp of approval; it meant I was good enough, smart enough, and people liked me. I no longer felt like I was on the outside looking in. I split my time between the main university campus and the affiliated veterans' hospital, and my practice was varied: doing anesthesia in the operating room; taking care of some of the sickest and most complicated patients on the planet in the ICU; teaching students, residents, and fellows from across a whole range of medical specialties; developing curricula and lectures; publishing research articles and book chapters; and leading small research studies. Beyond how it *felt* to be part of such a storied institution, the work itself was exactly what I wanted to be doing. Even so, as much as I was in love with the university and my work, I was still on my own. And for the first time in my life, at the age of thirty-six, this was beginning to gnaw at me.

But then I met someone. Her name was Jenica Cimino, and she was a research assistant in the ICU. I was sure she had been flirting with me for the past year or so, here and there, in passing conversations about travel or patients. One night when we were alone at a bank of computers in the ICU, I could feel it—she was going to finally ask me out. "This probably isn't appropriate for work," she began hesitantly.

Yes! I shouted silently to myself.

"And for all I know, you're already seeing someone," she continued.

Here it comes . . . I was so certain.

"But I've got this sister I think you'd like," she finished.

You know that *womp-womp* sound, the sad trombone? The disappointment I was feeling could have made a sound only like that. Before I could even muster up the courage to ask Jenica out myself, she was already telling me about Lindsey's résumé, probably assuming I'd be impressed by her academic pedigree: bachelor's from the University of Southern California, master's from the London School of Economics, a law degree from the University of California. Admittedly, I was now interested. I would find out later that Lindsey was mortified that this was how Jenica chose to describe her. But Jenica knew her audience. Physicians, especially academic ones, are embarrassingly prone to adoring these academic pyrotechnics.

An email exchange followed. Lindsey and I had plans to meet for coffee the Sunday after Thanksgiving, November 27, 2011. I found out later that she thought first dates should always be coffee because no one ever wants a second cup. *She's funny,* I thought, *and charming.* We met at The Grove in the Marina, which is the San Francisco neighborhood she lived in. I walked in and spotted her immediately. She was wearing black leggings and a nubby mustard sweater, and I thought she was super cute—and young. After introducing ourselves, I blurted out, "How old are you exactly?" Even I knew that was an odd thing to say, but I was immediately smitten and I was worried she was twenty-three or twenty-four, and at thirty-six I didn't want to revisit my twenties. Thankfully, she was thirty.

The date seemed to go well. Halfway through, she paused mid-sentence, thought for a second, cocked her head to the side, and said, "You know, I get the sense that *a lot* of women have put *a lot* of work into you." And then she smiled. What could I say? I knew she was right. Knowing her the way I do now, even though we probably laughed about it at the time, I know she didn't mean it as a joke. It occurred to her on some brain-stem, intuitive level not just that past relationships had taught me how to dress or how to act, which they certainly had, but also that something deeper had taken place over all those lonely, sad years. Without us ever explicitly talking about it, something about that comment made me feel understood, seen, and safe, and in that moment it also made me want to step up to be the ultimate version of myself, to put all those lessons learned from previous failed relationships to work. Still, I can't say that from this point on I completely opened up for Lindsey all my hidden compartments of pain and fear.

"I'm hungry," Lindsey said as we finished our coffee, thinking it'd be an obvious signal that she wanted to extend the date. It was not obvious to me, so I said, "Well, you're in luck! Look at all the places you can pick up takeout on your way home!" Apparently not enough women had put *quite* enough work into me just yet. We recovered, though, when she agreed to a ride home and when I dropped her off, I realized that we had practically walked past her apartment to get to my car, so I knew she was interested, too. On December 5, 2011, the entry in my calendar says "Cancel Match.com subscription."

Food was a regular theme in our dating life, in part because Lindsey had cooked professionally after law school and before starting her career in policy work, but also because she was surrounded by a large, boisterous Italian family that loved to cook. Whenever I was over at her parents' house, at breakfast we'd be talking about what we were making for lunch, and at lunch we'd talk about what we were going to make for dinner. Her parents had a loving marriage, they lived in a calm and happy home, and Lindsey had not grown up anxious about her father's temper, her mother's worries, or the lack of financial security, as I had.

Her dad almost immediately took me under his wing. A fellow Midwesterner, Michael saw in me many of the same things he knew about himself after having left home, leaving his family behind, and striking out on his own in California even as he maintained the earnestness and humility of someone who'd never left. He had only daughters, and I didn't have a father, and although two Midwesterners would never speak of it, I think we both felt like we were puzzle pieces that hadn't found their match until now. During one of our first meetings, he walked me through his recipe for roasting chickens stuffed with Meyer lemons and rosemary from his yard along with the stuffed artichokes that had been a Sicilian standby in his family for generations. It was the first time I had worn an apron, and I was so excited to put it on and be a part of this scene of familial joy and camaraderie. As we sat down at the table, I realized that save for those mushy pickled ones in a jar or can, I'd never actually eaten a whole artichoke before. If you've ever seen one on your plate, you know what my first impression was. They look positively prehistoric, and as though they'd be almost painful to eat. But from across the table, and without saying a word, I could see Michael trying to attract my attention without drawing it from others, as if to say, *I've been where you are. Watch me first. I'll show you, and then you'll know.* I felt looked after and safe.

Michael died of pulmonary fibrosis in 2018, two years before Pia and Isa were born. Within that same year, we had also lost two of his four siblings to the same condition, which is essentially a stiffening of the lungs until the patient suffocates to death. His older brother as well as his dad had died of pulmonary fibrosis years earlier. Researchers think it's genetic, but Michael had grown up in the 1950s in a small railroad town on the Iowa-Illinois border playing in rail yards rife with asbestos, working summers shoveling coal, and swimming in the Mississippi, which at that time glistened with runoff. We didn't know then what we know now about the impact of big industries on these small, remote towns. Some part of me, with zero expertise on this topic, always wondered: Was Michael's illness genetic or was it environmental? Just before he passed away, I held him on the hospital bed that had been wheeled into their family home and I told him that he was safe, his work was done, and he could go peacefully now. I'll never forget how he gazed up at me and nodded.

I look at photos of myself before and after meeting Lindsey and I realize that my whole life I'd only thought I'd been smiling in pictures. After meeting Lindsey, I could actually see that I was smiling a genuine grin, the kind where your eyes crease, your mouth is slightly open, and your cheeks almost hurt. Our wedding was intimate and lovely. Lindsey's dad had become ill by this point and we weren't sure how long he had. So on a whim we decided to skip off to Chicago on Valentine's Day weekend with just our parents, our siblings, and a group of thirty close friends. We chose Chicago because it was central for my friends and family, and we figured the California contingent would fly anywhere—and they did! Almost everyone showed up with just a few weeks' notice. Lindsey walked toward me to an acoustic version of "Here Comes the Sun" with her dad beaming by her side. We wrote our own vows and read them aloud; one of my best friends, Seth, became ordained so he could officiate. Our closest friends and siblings gave speeches, and then, as the night was winding down, my mom got up and opened the door to the private room we were in at the restaurant, The Little Goat, and called down the hall, "Okay, Martin, are you out there? We're ready!" In strode Martin Zellar, whose recordings my brother had introduced me to so many years ago, and the one whose music formed the soundtrack of my misspent twenties. I'd seen him from a barroom floor more times than I could count, and now he was standing right there in front of me, ready to play a few love songs for our wedding in what was a surreal, full-circle moment. It had been Jenica's idea initially, and Lindsey loved it; they tracked down Martin, who spent half the year in Mexico to escape the Midwest's winters. He happened to be in the Midwest that weekend and changed his flight to serenade us on our wedding night. I was blown away when he walked in, I had never been so surprised by anything in my life. I almost felt my heart stop, which isn't something a doctor says lightly.

I still keep in touch with this musical icon of mine, updating him about our milestones. A bit of wisdom he gave me after our Valentine's weekend wedding has always stuck with me:

> I'm sure that life has changed a great deal for you since February, and I'm sure it will continue to do so. I'm also sure that you'll find those changes to almost always be for the better. Some of them might take longer than others to adjust to, and a few you may never adjust to, but that's okay. Eso es amor (such is love)!

It was a whirlwind year. We got engaged and married; we bought our first home together, the middle of three flats in a Victorian built in1886 in the Haight-Ashbury neighborhood of San Francisco; Lindsey had started working at a company that was little known at the time, Uber; and I turned forty with an incredible birthday weekend in the Carmel Valley with all of my friends, who came out yet again to celebrate. I assumed that a pregnancy announcement would follow soon. But it didn't happen that year, or the year after, or even the year after that. It took over five years to conceive our twins. Nothing was ever medically "wrong," but clearly nothing was ever right.

At times I felt like I was back in the very mess of responsibility, trying and failing to care for Lindsey in the throes of fertility treatments, that I had spent my whole life trying to avoid. I would come home and instead of finding Lindsey on the couch with a washcloth on her forehead or ensconced in our bedroom with the shades drawn, she was just sad all the time, a shadow of her vibrant and vivacious self. A therapist once asked her if having babies would truly make her happy, almost insinuating that her desperation to have kids couldn't possibly be the reason for her despair. I still recall how quickly and confidently she replied "Yes" to the therapist's question: Having babies would in fact make her happy and fix her grief. It turned out that she was right: After Pia and Isa arrived, Lindsey was exuberant. Even buried in the sheer volume of work associated with infant twins, she never complained. It was astounding to me. And her experience was most certainly not mine. The cracks were starting to form. I might have been able to hide them from Lindsey still, but while we were in the thick of fertility treatment, I felt all the pain and anxiety of caring and worrying for someone else creeping back in. "Of course I want kids," I'd said in one of those early conversations when we were still feeling each other out. I was so attracted to Lindsey, I'd have said anything to keep the ball rolling, to keep her interest up. But did I *really* want them? Did I ache to be a father, to grope my way through unfamiliar territory, committing to a lifetime of accountability even though there was no road map? Or could I at least see some longer-term vision of experiencing the beauty of parenthood? I was so wrapped up in my own life, correcting, at least on a superficial level, those things I thought had been missing from my childhood: an enviable career, a beautiful girl on my arm, a glamorous lifestyle.

Adding to the sadness in those years was Lindsey's dad dying, too young. Toward the end of his life, before he was too sick, he and Ayn walked the Camino de Santiago, a Christian pilgrimage of more than five hundred miles through northern Spain. This experience was so moving and profound to them, as lifelong Catholics, that it defined their last years together. Oh, the love they had for it: the beauty, the spirituality, the friends, the sense of freedom. As her dad became sicker, Lindsey found her job becoming simultaneously more intense and less meaningful. She had stayed at Uber, through the pressures of working at what was then a start-up, only because of their full coverage of the fertility treatments. But watching her dad wither away before her eyes, coupled with the disappointment of our fertility journey, led her to quit her job in 2017 and suggest that she and I walk the Camino de Santiago ourselves. It was one of the few times when she sprang something like that on me out of the blue and I was on board immediately. In fact, I felt liberated. We borrowed gear from her parents—backpacks, trekking poles, and even clothes—and headed to Spain. The trip was a needed antidote to the way we'd been growing out of the closeness we'd felt before the fertility issues. And I wonder if we would have survived as a couple if we hadn't had that time away to bond before the kids arrived.

CHAPTER 5

TIME I HAD SOME TIME ALONE

I RECALL TAKING only one photo of Lindsey while she was pregnant, and it wasn't even my idea. Someone else requested the photo so that she could turn it into a Mother's Day card for Lindsey as a surprise for her very first Mother's Day. In hindsight, I wasn't full-blown panicking or depressed yet, but I was checked out. I remember thinking that now that she was actually pregnant, I would go from having one person to take care of to three. Visions of Lindsey lying on the couch with a washcloth on her forehead and our entire house shrouded in darkness, with all three of them crying, started to creep into my subconscious. The sense of responsibility started to overwhelm me, but I didn't talk to anyone about it, not Lindsey, not my close friends, and certainly not a professional. For the first time I wondered if this was how my dad had felt throughout our childhood until he couldn't stand it anymore and made his escape, never to be heard from again. Was this fear of responsibility and taking care of others in my genes? Was it inescapable? And what did it say about me that I couldn't bear the idea of taking care of my own family when every day I took care of very sick patients? All of this was swirling in my mind throughout Lindsey's pregnancy, but once the pandemic arrived, I blamed that for making me feel skittish, and I blamed my sense of unease on Lindsey's reluctance to do absolutely every single test, sonogram, and exam. No one seemed to notice any change in me, or at least that's what I told myself.

Very early in the AIDS outbreak, in the early 1980s, there was a group of physicians at UCSF who would ultimately establish the nation's first outpatient AIDS clinic, Ward 86, at the San Francisco General Hospital in 1983. President Ronald Reagan didn't proactively address AIDS until 1987, a full six years after the first known cases surfaced in San Francisco. Those early doctors were in a sense playing Russian roulette with their lives every day in those earliest years, because initially no one knew the cause of the disease or the route of transmission; they only knew that getting AIDS was a death sentence. And yet those early pioneers at Ward 86 woke up each day and took care of these patients, whom many in society considered pariahs, and then went home each night to spouses and young children. Having learned about this history,

I always thought that when push came to shove, I'd do the same. But when the COVID-19 pandemic hit hard and I was called to put on a mask and a simple paper gown each day and go into the ICU, I recall being afraid—afraid that I might catch it, that I might bring it home to my pregnant wife, and that my need and desire to do this kind of work might hurt my family. No one would've guessed, but whatever drove the fearlessness these Ward 86 doctors exhibited, I didn't have it, a realization that both surprised and disappointed me. As my confidence in my ability to be a father and even a husband began to falter, my confidence in my profession did the same. Even that hint of hesitation was enough to make me question the very person that I had worked so hard to become. Was I really the competent, heroic doctor I imagined myself to be? Then again, were any of us?

The subtle angst that gnawed at me throughout Lindsey's pregnancy only intensified with the girls' birth. There are pictures of us outside the hospital lobby as we are about to leave with the twins, the UCSF logo in the background, Lindsey carrying a vase of multicolored tulips, and the girls in their car seats, bundled up in knitwear handmade by family members. I'd handled everything else in life; I'd handle this, too. But behind the smile my brain was going into panic mode as I was forced to take on the reality that we were leaving the supportive environment of the hospital and I was not prepared. Instead of staying sheltered in the hospital, where every question had an answer and every cry was answered by a nurse, we were bound for the solitary environment of home, alone.

A few days before we left the hospital, I asked the coterie of nurses and lactation consultants that had assembled in our room what we needed to do to prepare to go home. I was being earnest, but they chuckled in response. I don't think they expected a competent doctor to ask such a basic question. When they saw that my expression didn't change, they stopped smiling and thought about it, conferring with one another. Ultimately they said we needed two things: a commercial-grade breast pump and a night nurse (also called a night doula). The commercial-grade pump was giant and heavy, with its own suitcase, and kind of expensive to rent. Finding a night doula was a bit trickier. I searched online and just started calling people. Most of the ones I found were old Irish ladies, often former nurses. Even though they were professional and competent yet kind, in the end I was drawn to a wisp of a human being, a fairy of sorts, who lived out in the hippie enclave of Fairfax: Ruby Neal.

Ruby was in her early seventies and of average height, though she couldn't have weighed more than a hundred pounds. She had a thick mane of wavy gray hair. She laughed easily, her sentences were enormously long, and one night she confessed to Lindsey in a dreamy voice and with a far-off look that when she died, she was really going to miss the moon. I was looking for a rule book that included sleep schedules, eating schedules, and sleep training. Ruby was anything but that, and yet I was drawn to her warmth and her intuition. She had been a therapist for years; I don't know what made her become a night doula, but she spoke "baby" better than she spoke "adult." I would ask her very specific questions, like when would we start sleep training and how the process would go. She would give me answers that were so long-winded and convoluted that eventually I just stopped asking her questions. But that took months because I was so desperate to have a captain for this baby ship.

Her philosophy was entirely different from mine, I would eventually discover. She essentially felt that babies were just wired to do their thing and she was there to help us get on board and in sync with their schedule. That sounded crazy to me, but both our babies were sleeping through the night by four months and their weights were well into the 70th and 80th percentiles for singletons (twins usually weigh less), so it was hard to argue with her approach—and yet the results didn't assuage my fears and anxiety. I kept trying to systematize anything I could get my hands on, probably as a way to exhibit mastery and control over this seemingly wild and uncontrollable thing. One night I asked Ruby if we should really pick up the babies if they were crying; wouldn't it train them to cry more? She laughed and told me that they were only three months old, and they weren't manipulating us or trying to game the system. "They're just *babies,* Chris!" she exclaimed cheerfully. That provided me zero relief; there was nothing "just" about the girls.

Before Ruby arrived, though, Lindsey and I depended on a ragtag family team of amateurs. The first night home from the hospital was like a sleepover party. Ayn met us at the house because she recalled having come home to an empty home herself after giving birth to Lindsey and it had made her sad; she wanted us to be surrounded by family that first night. She brought us homemade chicken pot pie and tomatoes from the garden. We were all up throughout the night, soldiering on, while everything was novel and the sleep deprivation was still something we could joke about, like pulling an all-nighter in college. There are even pictures of me bringing Lindsey breakfast in bed on a fancy tray that first morning, light streaming in from the bay window, casting her in an angelic glow. In the picture she's smiling; she even took a bath after breakfast. There were no such pictures from subsequent mornings. As the days and nights wore on and blended together, the mix of exhaustion, disorientation, and frustration with the inscrutable needs of newborns began to take its toll on me.

I decided to take control of what I thought was becoming an out-of-control situation. I made a spreadsheet, one that looked like an ICU flow sheet, that tracked the twins' wake and sleep cycles, when the babies ate and how much, and their poop and pee. I even had a little notepad by each side of the bed so that if Lindsey happened to feed them while I slept, she could manually enter the data that I would then transfer to the spreadsheet. I had a million good reasons for tracking all this biodata: Were they eating enough? Were they staying hydrated? Which one hadn't had a wet diaper in four hours? Ayn and Lindsey couldn't stop smirking. But I felt I was brilliant. I was exhibiting mastery over something that was totally chaotic. When we went to that first pediatrician's appointment, the girls had already gained their birth weight back and then some. With that outcome, however, the spreadsheet immediately became obsolete, and I recall grappling for other solutions I could come up with given my professional tool kit.

On the third day home from the hospital, Ayn left and my friend and former colleague Kathy came in from the Peninsula (the area south of the city of San Francisco) to act as night nurse. Kathy was an operating room nurse by training. She originally hailed from South Philadelphia; she loved the Jersey shore, she was wry, and she had great quips. She'd say "What's a girl gotta do to get a drink around here?" when Pia cried in hunger, or "Where's the plug?" when she was looking for a pacifier to give to Isa. And she always brought mountains of baked goods. Kathy had recently lost her husband, Brian, also my friend and colleague, to ALS. She'd raised her own two daughters more than two decades prior and knew the ropes. When I think of her and those early days, I cry. She'd laugh if she knew I was getting sentimental, or at the very least minimize it, but she was my only tether to anything real in those early days. She spoke "parent," she spoke "medical professional," and she spoke "mom." Plus, she was in a sense mine—something wonderful *I* was bringing to the table. This was during the pandemic, and almost nobody was visiting us, which made Kathy's visits even more heroic. She was funny, sarcastic, and confident, but she was also my confidant. She was probably the first person to hint that something might be wrong with me, but I didn't catch those hints, and now I can recall her comments only in hindsight.

On one of these early nights with Kathy, Lindsey started to become delirious with fevers and shaking chills. I essentially told Lindsey to pull it together because we had a guest, which was a cruel thing to say. But what was really going through my mind was that she had an abscess in her abdomen that was the cause of the fevers—or, worse yet, that she had a new source of internal bleeding. The very thing I'd dreaded while she was in the ICU, having an endlessly sick wife to take care of, seemed to be becoming a reality, and my mind was racing to worst-case scenarios. Then Lindsey started to faint from the fevers. Kathy had to suggest I take Lindsey to the hospital. So, only a few days after we had checked out of the hospital, we were right back in it, and I was scared. I hastily dropped Lindsey off at the curb while I parked, because I wasn't able to think straight. When I headed in, I saw Lindsey wandering around the lobby, disoriented because of the fever, and I had to lead her up to the proper floor. It turned out Lindsey had mastitis, an infection in the breasts' milk ducts, which ended up plaguing her off and on almost the entire time she breastfed. She would find things that alleviated it, like a lot of hot showers and sunflower lecithin, but exclusively breastfeeding twins took a toll on her body. The fact that I didn't recognize this, didn't even think to look it up, was unlike me; on top of that, chastising Lindsey was downright cruel. I was usually patient, almost to a fault. But that night I was annoyed and even a bit angry, and underneath it all was fear. What had I gotten myself into? They say that having children cracks all your old wounds wide open, but at this point I didn't know that saying, and I didn't have the wherewithal to even recognize what was happening. I just thought this was one huge inconvenience that would pass if I continued to develop systems to master it and get everyone under control. Michael once said that Jenica had been "the ultimate quartermaster" when he, Jenica, and Lindsey had trekked a small portion of the Pacific Crest Trail years earlier. That had stuck in my mind; now I was going to be this team's quartermaster.

Then on September 9, 2020, we all woke up to darkness. We'd been up and down all night, as usual, so when I saw that my watch said ten o'clock, I was so disoriented that I wasn't sure if it was ten in the morning or ten at night. Wildfires had been raging across California for weeks, and then Oregon was ablaze as well, and the huge number of wildfires in both states combined with unusual air circulation patterns created what we would come to know as "Orange Day." Photos of the Bay Area in this eerie extraterrestrial haze inundated every news outlet all over the world that day, but in my mind it was more like the world around us was echoing my roiling, collapsing mental state. The orange skies were visually dramatic and bizarre to actually live through, and yet when Ayn mentioned it to me that morning—a perfectly innocuous comment—as I sat trying to calm the girls, I remember being so rattled I could only shout, "I can't do anything about the sky right now, Ayn!" For me, this moment marked the first time of many where I could feel the limits of my ability to cope, where I could feel myself losing control.

That same day we had to drive across the Golden Gate Bridge to a pediatrician's appointment in Mill Valley. The apocalyptic vibrations of that day reverberated within me, heightening the sense of intensity and disorientation I was feeling inside. Our own circadian rhythms were already a mess, with the girls waking up at alternating three-hour intervals, and that day something about seeing streetlights on in the middle of the day was just enough to push me right to the edge. I was distracted, I was anxious, and I couldn't think straight, at least not straight enough to manage what was happening or what needed to happen, with any degree of patience or poise. I was short with Lindsey, trying to get things to happen faster. I yelled. I sounded annoyed, I'm sure. With Ayn's help, though, we managed to get the girls loaded into the car in the midst of what seemed like combat or an alien invasion. The appointment itself went well. I overheard the pediatrician asking Lindsey kindly how she was doing. It was clear she was asking about Lindsey's well-being, but out of the blue Lindsey said something along the lines of "I'm okay, but I'm worried about my husband. He doesn't seem like himself." I'm not sure if any ICU doctor during the pandemic would be themselves, but I had the added stress of being a new father to twins, and now the sky was orange. It was midday at this point, and instead of getting lighter out, it was actually getting darker; the orange was turning crimson. I listened with half an ear from my seat by the door, away from the conversation. "Maybe he should join a men's group," the pediatrician suggested, but she didn't have any particular ones to recommend immediately. Even though I was right there, this pediatrician—an older doctor in private practice, nearing retirement—didn't turn to me and ask about my well-being or mental state. Not that I would have said anything other than "I'm fine," most likely. Like when my friend Greg had, months earlier, given me the book on how to be a father, I felt slightly indignant. I didn't need to join a group to talk about my feelings. I think I felt like the real problem was with everyone else. Veterans who have lived with short military haircuts, pressed uniforms, and polished boots for years often talk about how when they leave the service and reenter the civilian world, everyone else looks so messy, almost dirty. In that moment, I thought that everyone else was being messy and casual; I thought there were real solutions to this chaos and disorder, and we just hadn't fully tapped into them yet. But at this point I was nothing if not determined to crack the code.

A few days later, I victoriously announced to Kathy the ultimate solution for not getting bored while I was rocking the babies. I'd decided in my head that the perfect tempo for rocking or bouncing them was 103 beats per minute, the tempo of REM's "It's the End of the World as We Know It (And I Feel Fine)." I had looked up the lyrics on the internet so I could sing them in my head and mouth them silently as I rocked the girls to sleep, whether it was the middle of the night, bedtime, or nap time. It seemed creative and resourceful to me at the time, but in hindsight it was an awful theme to have running in my head. Or maybe it was an accurate reflection of my own subconscious, and the most honest thing in front of me. I had been lamenting to Kathy how inefficient the process of putting babies to sleep was; what was I supposed to do during these seemingly interminable sessions, multiple times a day? "I don't know, Chris," she said in her dry, monotone, Jersey-accented voice. "Maybe just rock your babies to sleep like everyone else." The fact that billions of people over many millennia had done this before us and emerged unscathed provided me no comfort; the thought literally hadn't even entered my head, because I was just racing to fix things, to put out what I saw as fires.

At the next pediatrician's appointment, maybe two months in, around October, 2020, I wasn't as optimistic about cracking the code with supposedly intelligent solutions like spreadsheets and the perfect rocking tempo. I could tell Lindsey was getting a bit weary of my anxious energy.

I couldn't help saying that I thought there was something wrong with one of our twins, as she cried all the time.

"Babies cry," was all the pediatrician said.

But I thought this felt different, and I tried to convince her. "No, but this is really bad."

"Yes, yes, some kids cry, and it's really terrible."

"Yeah, but this is like there's something wrong, like the sound is bloodcurdling."

"Yes, to feel like the cry is bloodcurdling, that's normal."

"Normal?"

"Yes, sometimes it's really terrible," she replied. We were starting to sound like an Abbott and Costello comedy sketch.

"Terrible? Isn't that what I said?"

"Is it?"

"But . . . can't somebody *do* something?"

"Maybe it's colic."

"Okay, colic, I've heard of that," I said. Finally we were getting somewhere, a real diagnosis for what was happening here.

"Colic is when your baby cries a lot."

"Yes, but from what?" I wanted to know.

"Nobody knows. Colic is frequent, prolonged, and intense crying in an otherwise healthy infant," she said, essentially repeating out loud the medical definition.

I couldn't believe it, they had come up with a term that does nothing except just that: give you a word to hang on to but no action to take. She was saying that babies cry, sometimes a lot, and we don't always know why, but it almost always gets better. The subtext I took away was that I needed to toughen up or distract myself. But for me, these were the kind of cries that seemed to pull on wires connected directly into my soul and jolt the very foundation of my being. Was she sick? In pain? Was something wrong? Should we be doing something? In response to these guttural wails, I felt paralyzed, though my heart was racing. That the cries came unpredictably and were nearly impossible to control sparked a fear in me, another stirring of something even deeper: I could not care for my daughters.

The reality, though, was that it wasn't much better for me when they were happy, either. One day we were all up the street at Grattan Playground, enjoying a rare afternoon of San Francisco sun, with the girls lying on blankets on the ground, and Kathy, Lindsey, and I surrounding them. Something we did made one of them laugh, and then the other one smiled. It was cute, fun, something out of the daily infant routine—the kind of thing that reminds you why you struggle through all of this, because eventually it gets better and in the meantime you catch glimpses of joy. But my reaction was quite different. I mumbled out loud something like "What do they even have to be happy about?" It's easy to hate myself for thinking this, let alone saying it, but it's so clear to me now that I was not well. "Okay, Debbie Downer," Kathy commented drolly. "We're not going to invite you to the party anymore."

The daily grind of poor sleep, unpredictability, and weeks of holding babies all day was taking a toll. I was developing a constant pit in my stomach, an anxious gnawing that would not yield. In casual conversation with colleagues or friends in which I would lament my day-to-day existence, they'd reply with things like "Men don't really like newborns, pal." Another comment I would get was that I had "the baby blues." Or they'd say I was simply missing my old life, like I just didn't have enough time to go to the gym or shoot the shit with my friends. Or they'd say I was merely tired from all the work of caring for the girls—"All those diapers!" It wasn't that; I could've changed a million diapers and heated a million bottles. This was different. This was elemental. Something was happening inside me that wasn't right. The crack I'd started to feel when Lindsey was pregnant was becoming wider, and I couldn't stop the damage from spreading.

Lindsey, on the other hand, felt as blessed as she had anticipated, reveling in the very things that were driving me mad, and if she could tell or sense what was going on with me, she didn't say it with words. But her body language was starting to communicate something beyond the stress of parenthood, and more akin to annoyance that my behavior was adding to it.

Later, on Easter Sunday, more than six months after the babies were born, I was lying on the bed in our guest room and lifting Pia in the air, high above my head and somewhat playfully, with a smile on my face as Pia smiled down at me. Jenica, who'd been staying with us since November after a breakup, quickly grabbed her camera and took a dozen or so photos—because, she said, it was the first time since the twins were born that she had seen me play with them, do something a little bit silly. Think about all the big and little things that parents typically do with infants from the time they are born, like tickling them, making ridiculous noises, blowing raspberries on their bellies, calling them silly names, or making up even sillier songs. Jenica hadn't seen me do a single one of those things until now. She told me later that one of her first memories after moving in with us was sitting around with me in the living room. She understandably wanted to talk about the babies, but I kept changing the subject to anything else—music, my wine collection, the state of the world—until finally I snapped at her, "I don't even understand how new parents can love their babies. They're like aliens." This hit Jenica hard. Her bond with the girls went beyond being their only aunt. When Lindsey and I were in the thorniest part of our infertility journey, after multiple courses of IVF had failed, Jenica had come to us with an offer to give us her eggs. I think I said yes before Lindsey did, in one of those split-second things that just immediately and instinctually felt right. The way I rationalized it to myself, though, was that if Jenica had children and something happened to her, Lindsey and I would raise them, and of course she'd do the same for us. This felt as natural to me as anything else we'd done to that point, and for reasons we'll never know it worked. There's a lot I blocked out from those early months, but I've never been able to block out the look on Jenica's face when I called them "aliens," as though I'd turned her extraordinary gift into something base, something ugly. It was a stark illustration of how tormented I'd been from almost the minute they were born.

When we knew Lindsey was pregnant we'd agreed that I would take five months off from work after the babies arrived. But after they were born I argued—to myself, mostly—that the hospital needed me sooner. After all, this was still the early stages of the pandemic; all over the nation, hospital hallways and conference rooms had been converted into ICUs, multiple patients were being hooked up to a single ventilator, field hospitals were being set up in unconventional places like Central Park in New York City. Approaching the UCSF hospital was like entering a war zone. Tents and temporary buildings had been set up outside, the main entrances were barricaded, and to get in you had to go through a gauntlet of temperature checkers and intake screeners. It didn't resemble my professional home in any way, but I assumed that the sense of purpose and ease of returning to what I know how to do best would assuage the anxiety I was feeling at home. Certainly there was no more noble cause in the world just then than treating COVID patients. It was moments like this that intensivists trained for. Instead, though, I started to see little reminders of Lindsey's time in the ICU, of our time in the hospital, and the traumatic birth we'd survived. It started with, of all things, the napkin on a patient's meal tray that I noticed as I was leaving the room. It was a particular shade of bright yellow. These were the same yellow napkins we'd had in the ICU in Labor and Delivery, which was located at an entirely different UCSF campus. As I paused and stared down at this napkin, my heartbeat began to quicken. Slowly I backed out of the patient's room and into the hallway, only to encounter a half dozen more meal carts crowding the passageway. They all had crumpled versions of this same yellow napkin on it. I started to walk faster, trying to escape this scene, my heart now racing, my pace quickening into a run toward the bathroom at the end of the hall. I rushed in, locked myself in a stall, and sat on the closed toilet seat taking deep breaths, arms extended, hands on my knees. Eventually I got up from the toilet seat and went out to wash my face with cold water. Thankfully the bathroom was empty as I looked in the mirror and silently gave myself a little pep talk: *You can do this; don't be like Will.*

In telling myself that, I was going back to an incident that had occurred years earlier, on the very last day of my last year of my residency. On that day I was woken up at four in the morning by a code blue. When a patient's heart has stopped or is about to stop, anyone who is observing this shouts out to people around them, "Call a code blue!"; alternatively, they can pick up a phone and dial an internal emergency number that in turn initiates a repeated call over the loudspeaker: "Code blue in room 208!" When this happens, a designated team of doctors, nurses, and respiratory therapists must stop everything they are doing and go to room 208. While the specifics vary from hospital to hospital, at UCSF the senior resident on the cardiology team working that day is assigned to lead that team. That person always wears black scrubs. The other people assigned to be a part of the code blue team at UCSF include an ICU nurse, an administrative nurse, an anesthesiologist, a resident from anesthesiology, a person from transport, a member of the hospital police, a chaplain, and a social worker. It's basically everyone who would be involved if a person was dying—because essentially a person *is* dying.

So on this very last overnight shift of my anesthesia residency, I was woken up by the overhead speaker blaring and my pager buzzing, letting me know that there was a code blue in the cardiac ICU. The sun was just beginning to come up when I rushed into the room along with the rest of the code blue team. In the ICU bed was a young woman sitting up and gasping for breath, and I saw that she was visibly pregnant. I quickly learned this patient had a form of heart failure that there is very little we can do about; in these patients, even the smallest changes in medication can lead to cardiac arrest. The code blue team decided "Caroline" needed to be sedated and intubated so that the cardiology team could insert an intra-aortic balloon pump to support her heart. The attending physician, Dr. Klafta, someone I idolized, began the process of intubating her, while I, kneeling on the hard ICU floor, inserted a needle and catheter into the radial artery in her wrist. But then her heart stopped altogether, which means the baby stopped getting any blood flow as well. The obstetricians immediately cut into her lower abdomen for an emergency C-section, and I started to do chest compressions for CPR. Even an athlete can do good-quality CPR for only a minute or two at maximum, because it's so physical; soon the person giving CPR starts to fade, and with that loss of strength comes a loss of effectiveness. I always say that if you're not breaking ribs while you're doing CPR, especially on older people, you're not doing CPR correctly. So when someone else took over the CPR and I stepped back, I saw the obstetrics team pull out the baby. She was unimaginably small, well under two pounds, and blue. Blue meant she'd been without oxygen for a while. They immediately put the baby in one of those clear heated bassinets and whisked her out of the room. And then, almost miraculously, Caroline stabilized. She wasn't better; she just wasn't actively dying any longer. The code team dispersed; I was one of the last ones out of the room, and even before I exited the room I heard out in the hall a deep and inconsolable sobbing. It was her husband, Will. It was a Saturday morning, so the hospital was nearly empty, which just amplified the sound. I later found out that Caroline died a few hours later. I never found out what happened to Will or their new baby girl, but his grief had stayed with me, buried all these years until, like him, I was faced with the prospect of my wife dying in childbirth, and raising these girls without the mother that wanted them like she wanted air to breathe. And it was this flashback, this damned yellow napkin, so specific in its color, that unearthed that horrific memory and brought it into real life right in front of me.

As I stood in front of the bathroom mirror at UCSF all those years later, I kept saying to myself, *Don't lose it like Will, buddy. You can hold it together.* My hands gripped the sides of the sink until my knuckles were white, and I took deep, long breaths.

A few minutes later I walked out of that bathroom and checked on my next patient, a thirty-three-year-old developmentally disabled woman who had been admitted from a care facility up north with septic shock. Even though she was an adult, the notes described her as having a mental age of three. I observed that she was moaning and writhing slightly, the way a very sick and uncomfortable child would. She started to cry and told me she was afraid. I had to insert an arterial blood pressure monitor, which meant that I had to do a small but painful procedure. Even though she was an adult, I spoke to her the way I would to a small child, as she clutched a stuffed unicorn, and we managed to get through it. But I was shaken from the experience in a way I had never been before in my time in medicine. When I took off my sterile gown and left the room, I ran into Liz, a social worker who had been at UCSF for over forty years. When she'd first moved to San Francisco in the 1960s, she and her friends squatted in an abandoned house in Pacific Heights, the same neighborhood where mansions today regularly sell for $15 million. She still has that countercultural, irreverent quality about her, and she's also incredibly competent and smart. She's always at the hospital late into the evening, not catching up on paperwork but actually with patients. I was relieved to see her, and we talked about the patient I had just seen; I think I wanted to encourage Liz to check on this patient and her family. But as I began to describe the situation, I started to cry. I kept imagining Pia and Isa like this, suffering, alone, and vulnerable. And then my mind wandered to the inevitability of that patient's parents' death; when they died, who was going to take care of her? She was absolutely defenseless, with the only shield between her and the system, her and the hospital, her and the world, those gray-haired parents who looked so tired and worried and old. She had no siblings; after her parents died, there'd be nothing to buffer her from what felt like a cruel, miserable world.

It's true what they say: Once you have children, you see

your kids in everything and everyone. Every vulnerable adult patient was someone's baby at some point, and I felt my ability to handle this reality unraveling. "I'm not sure I can work in the ICU anymore," I told Liz. She was visibly startled; we had done a lot of family meetings together over the years, and she often specifically requested me to lead them. She tried to assuage my worries: The patient clutching a unicorn would be fine, because her parents weren't that old and the family had resources. She also tried to remind me that moments like this were just part of ICU work. But none of this mattered to me, as my mind just kept going to the worst-case scenario. Interestingly, especially for a social worker, she never asked me why I'd had such a sudden change of heart, what was going on that would precipitate this change, or even simply if I was okay or wanted to talk. I don't think it's common for doctors to suddenly announce to a colleague they have just randomly run into that they are considering leaving a practice, but even that didn't seem to raise any red flags to her. To be fair, even I didn't know how quickly things were deteriorating for me; all I knew was that not only couldn't I handle being at home, but I also now didn't like how it felt to be at my job in the ICU.

My work had been the most important thing in my life, and right in front of my eyes, it was changing from something difficult merely mentally and physically, comforting in its cold precision, to something emotionally devastating. Changing, too, from a respite from home, and all the anxiety and unpredictability that came with it, into its own source of angst; home was impossible and work was becoming impossible. Ayn was probably the first to see it: "You're falling apart, unraveling; your identity is changing," she'd say. "This will be the making of you, if you can let it in."

If I can let it in, I thought, *can I even survive it?*

I didn't know what to do with this new feeling taking over my previously unaffected doctor mind. Was working in the ICU, something that was so central to my sense of self and self-worth, maybe actually bad for me? Would I keep doing it? Like a lot of hard things during that time, I stuffed those feelings down, knowing I had to get through the shift. But as I walked home at the end of that day, I was glad to be outside the walls of the hospital but feared what awaited me inside the walls at home. So when I got back to the house, instead of going inside I went to the closed garage, got in my car, and just sat there. Over the previous few months the garage had become a dark hole, a place where my mind would race with all the possibilities of problems, but the only resolution to those problems it could conceive of was death: not mine, but theirs. In those moments, unconstrained by pretense or decorum, I'd imagine all three of them dead from a car crash. When Lindsey had been out with the twins, often at her mom's, I'd call or text when I thought they'd be on their way back; when I didn't hear back right away, that would be my very first thought, or maybe my very first wish—that there'd been a car crash, everyone was gone, and I was free. But that worked only if they all died. I'd consider all the options silently in that dark garage: What if only one of the girls survived? Could I handle that? What if just Lindsey died? How on earth could I handle both of the children? Or what if just the girls died and Lindsey lived? Would living with my wife's unfathomable grief be something I could handle? I didn't share any of these thoughts with Lindsey until sometime later, when I was months removed from the worst of it. I don't know how she would've felt in the moment, but after the fact she said she wasn't surprised. I do know, though, that she likes to protect me from the worst of her fears. If she worried for her own safety, she never let on. If she worried that my acknowledgment of my thoughts regarding the death of her and the girls somehow signaled I had been even worse off than she'd feared, she kept that to herself.

CHAPTER 6

NO LAUGHING MATTER

WITHIN SIX MONTHS after the twins were born, Lindsey turned forty and I turned forty-six. It was still the height of the pandemic, so no one was actually doing much and it was a sad time to have a birthday, but for mine Lindsey and Jenica had this funny last-minute idea to do a blind taste test of my favorite foods in both lowbrow and highbrow versions and we'd all rank which one was better. Each course was paired with a beverage. So, for example, they did a fried chicken course, with fried chicken from both Popeye's and Nopa (an expensive, near-Michelin-quality place that, like many during the pandemic, had pivoted to takeout); the chicken was accompanied by White Claw for the former and a vintage champagne for the latter. We did a handful of such pairings; each of us would rank the dishes blind, and at the end we'd compare notes. Oh—and everyone had to show up in 1970s attire because I was born in 1975. And by everyone I mean Lindsey, Jenica, me, and our friend DeWolf. For the final course, DeWolf was going to cook aged rib eyes that he had been storing in the personal meat locker he'd built during the pandemic. Plus, it was a surprise. So when all this got rolled out, I had to pretend that I was thrilled, despite my worries about the noise waking the girls. At this point I had become so obsessed with the girls' sleep schedules that my nerves were frayed with fear around any activity that might wake them.

Just the week prior, Lindsey and I had taken a walk with the girls in Golden Gate Park to Stowe Lake, maybe a mile from the house. It was a sunny late afternoon, coming on the tail of several weeks in a row of fog and cold, as well as several months in a row of the city still feeling shut down and afraid because of the COVID pandemic. The combination of these things created the perfect storm for JFK Drive in Golden Gate Park to feel like a party. This main artery through Golden Gate Park had been closed to cars ever since the start of the pandemic, and it was like the entire city got the memo: Today was *the* day to celebrate. All of this within a city that has a history of elaborate Gay Pride parades, Fleet Week festivities, a bluegrass festival that takes over a hearty portion of the more than one thousand acres of the park, and the Bay to Breakers footrace, which is famous for its costumes, like teams running the course backward dressed as salmon swimming upstream. This random Sunday felt like an amalgam of these festive traditions, our very own Carnivale. But even with all of this joy and fun swirling around us, I couldn't get my head beyond the fact that the girls' nap was fast approaching. In fact, I was checking my watch obsessively. and as each minute passed my heartbeat began to quicken until I felt like my heart was going to explode out of my chest. I prodded Lindsey to think about starting to head back, a prodding that was met with "Let's do a lap around the lake," something that would add at least a half hour to our trip home. "I really think we need to head back sooner than that," I said. "They woke up early, so they'll need to nap earlier than usual. If they're overtired when we put them down to nap, they'll wake up even earlier. I really think that tiredness begets tiredness. I read this article the other day about the precise optimal wake window. . . ." I was talking fast now, trying to make my case. Surely, I thought, she'd see the wisdom in my logic and feel the same sense of impending panic I did, but nope. She was smiling and starting to tune me out, I could tell, which infuriated me even more. I was starting to hate her. I really was. I wanted her to be as anxious as I was so that she'd see I was right about getting control over all these things and therefore get on board with my systems. Yet here she was actually *enjoying* her life!

Sometime after I had abandoned the spreadsheet in the early weeks after the twins' birth, I retreated to the land of online sleep blogs, a series of forums dedicated to helping parents master their kids' sleep. These blogs are written by actual trained sleep experts, and they advise things like "If your kid wakes up early from their first nap, start the second nap earlier by half the amount of time of their early waking from the first nap." They threw around acronyms wildly, like DWT (desired wake time), WW (wake window), MOTN (middle-of-the-night waking), and EMW (early-morning waking). I first got hooked when someone wrote in about their twins' nap schedule and a moderator wrote back the following:

> Hey there. Are they 7.5 months adjusted, or closer to 8 mos adjusted? As written your schedule follows 3/3.5/4 [referring to 3-, 3.5-, and 4-hour wake windows] which isn't a recommended schedule. Did you move to 2 naps 6 weeks ago? Does daycare offer naps at a certain time? Are they offering 2 or more naps? Does the sleep report [from daycare] tell you when the last nap finishes?

These people were precise, with schedules down to single minutes. When I first found this forum, I was in the nursery with Jenica and Lindsey, and I started to read these responses out loud to get a laugh from them. They did laugh, but then Jenica said she was surprised *I* was laughing because this actually seemed right up my alley. I brushed it off, scoffing, "No way, these people are even crazier than I am!" But then later that day I went back to the secret comfort of reading their acronyms and numerical breakdowns of how to produce the ultimate sleeping child. This was like version 2.0 of my spreadsheet-wielding, ideal-rocking-tempo self. I'd taken my need for control to the next level by becoming a part of a community of other people like myself because, ultimately, I wanted peace and didn't know any other way to find it than externally. If I am honest with myself now, if Lindsey had been just as obsessed with any of this as I was, it would have momentarily, superficially made me feel better, but my childhood pain, my yearning for control, would have reared its ugly head in some other way.

In the end, I felt I did not have a partner in the quest to control the chaos around us, and that made me increasingly angry and annoyed with Lindsey. I imagine she would say that at that time she did not have a partner in bonding with our children or taking any kind of joy in parenthood, which made her become distant from me. The epitome of self-centeredness, I was sure that I was suffering this imbalance more than she was.

So you can only imagine, then, how I responded when during our blind-taste-test birthday party DeWolf's attempt to cook the aged rib eyes on an absolutely smoking hot cast-iron pan triggered the smoke alarms in our house. I was furiously running around in my velour leisure suit and waving someone's suede fringed jacket in the air trying to put the alarms out when DeWolf's rayon tie caught fire, which then set off the alarms all over again. I was pissed. Anyone else would have found this beyond comical, especially after a year of shelter-in-place and social distancing; by this point, people were being vaccinated, en masse, and we hadn't yet realized that doing so didn't eliminate the threat. To boot, the girls never woke up. But that didn't change my resolve to never throw a party again. At the time, I thought that was a very reasonable response.

When Jenica had moved in, in November 2020, I'd actually been looking forward to having another person in the house. I thought, *Finally someone will see what I am seeing and help me get things under control here.* And because Jenica and Lindsey were very close, I thought I would have someone on my team who could talk to Lindsey about how her casualness was affecting everyone and having dire consequences for the family. Affecting everyone how, I couldn't exactly say. What those dire consequences were, I didn't exactly know. But I was convinced that Jenica would be an excellent referee, our problems would be solved, and I could go back to feeling better. When Jenica first moved in, it felt like a holiday. Lindsey would make elaborate homemade dinners, I would sit at the head of the table and deliberate over which bottle of wine to open, and we'd have a lively conversation. To me it felt like the times before we had babies. It never crossed my mind that Lindsey had been taking care of babies all day *and* feeding them *and* making this meal. Once dinner was ready, I would show up, and for a few hours a day I had relief from my anxiety, my stress, my deep sorrow, and my feelings of being stuck—as long as the girls were asleep.

A few weeks into these dinners, Lindsey pulled up an old *New York Times* article entitled "The 36 Questions That Lead to Love." Someone would pick a question, and we'd all share our answers. Mind you, it was the pandemic. You could not eat at restaurants, we weren't really going to people's homes, and when you have infant twins you are already in baby jail of sorts, so I think Lindsey was trying to change things up a bit. The questions ranged from "What would constitute a perfect day for you?" to "If you were to die this evening with no opportunity to communicate with anyone, what would you most regret not having told someone? Why haven't you told them yet?" I hated these questions. I felt exposed, under a microscope, and often I couldn't come up with much of an answer. I would have preferred to get drunk, something I'd been doing more and more at dinner, and make small talk. I recall one question: If I received a death sentence, how would I change how I was living? I wanted to shout, "I would get the fuck out of here and never look back!," but of course I couldn't say that, so I made up a benign answer and sprinkled in a few jokes. One night the question was about each person's most treasured memory. Lindsey went, then Jenica went, and then it was my turn. I had nothing. "Your wedding?" Jenica asked. "A favorite concert?" Lindsey asked. I kept making jokes and deflecting, but it's pretty hard to make jokes about your most treasured memory, and it's even harder to deflect when it's only three people sitting at a table. They eventually stopped prompting me with suggestions, exchanged a knowing look between themselves, and then started to clear the table. When Jenica left the dining room, Lindsey turned to me and said out of the blue, "Were you abused as a child?" I was shocked; this seemed to come out of left field. What exactly was she getting at? "I—I don't think so," I stammered, and the topic died of stilted silence. Eventually, Jenica returned and we resumed our stiff posture of awkward embarrassment and irritation. To be honest, I hadn't thought much about my childhood up until that point. I had spent my whole life trying to forget a lot of the feelings that marked my childhood, and I hadn't ever connected my experience of being a father now to my own childhood. It probably sounds crazy, but even though I'd wondered when the girls were born whether my own feelings mimicked my father's feelings when I was born, I didn't connect his abandonment with my struggles as a father now; all the things about him that made him a crummy father gave me the freedom to think I was better off without him, and that I was fine. My childhood was the past; whatever was happening now was something different, I was certain.

The thing about depression is that the experience is so much more vivid than the list of symptoms on a page. The list says "anhedonia," no longer taking joy in things, but the experience of it is more like wearing glasses that made everything around me look twisted and ugly. To not be able to even think of one treasured memory meant that I was seeing my own life through a warped lens. My brain was talking me out of what I thought was treasured and telling me it wasn't really that treasured. For example, when we had a question about our greatest accomplishment, that should have been a slam dunk for me. It didn't even have to be emotional; I had lots and lots of accomplishments to choose from. But every time I went to answer that night, I paused and eventually rejected my answer internally. My thought process went as follows: I couldn't say "finishing medical school" because I had failed my first quiz. I couldn't say "being a father" because what had I really done? I couldn't say "working at UCSF" because I'd been hired during a time in the economy when they must have been desperate. It went like that with each of those thirty-six questions. So I said nothing or made a joke, and therefore my answers were ugly and demonstrated how detached I was from everyone else. That ugliness wasn't what was in me, but it was all I could see, and therefore it was all that would come out.

In order to escape all these terrible thoughts in my head, I craved not only control but also a sense of freedom. When I was a kid, my third-grade class did a project on the albatross. It's a monogamous bird; the female lays a single egg once a year, and both the male and the female take turns sitting on the egg. Once the fledgling has hatched, the mother and father take off separately for over a year at sea, returning to that exact same nesting spot the following year—or sometimes two or even three years later—to repeat the process all over again. The albatross can be at sea for months or even years without ever touching land. I had been thinking lately a lot about this bird, mostly because I was consumed with the notion of feeling free and the idea of being at sea for months or even years spoke to me.

I started taking long, meandering walks on Haight Street, a mecca of street life. Small groups of unhoused men and women, always with dogs (likely for security as well as companionship), sometimes with guitars, often begging for cash or beer, occasionally selling homemade art or hand-beaded jewelry, were everywhere. Before COVID, Haight-Ashbury had already been infamous as a destination for the itinerant. But during the peak of the pandemic, with everyone who could hide in their homes doing so, the area felt like almost a scene from *Mad Max*. Instead of feeling bad for them or feeling thankful I had a roof over my head and financial stability, I felt the insane feeling of envy. I actually wanted to trade places with them. I craved what they seemingly had: solitude, freedom, no responsibility. With no one to answer to and seemingly no one to miss them, they could just pick up and go to another main street, or another county, or even another state. As I walked down Haight Street, I would imagine what part of the park I would sleep in, where I'd get my water, and whether

I'd be a solo homeless person or part of a group (definitely solo). The walks ended, maybe half the time or more, at one of the many bars on Haight: The Gold Cane, Hobson's Choice, Murio's, especially when the walks were at night, while Lindsey was putting the girls to sleep. Outdoor tables at bars were one upside to pandemic life: I could drink and smoke at the same time, the same refuge of drugs I'd see in those on the street, and one I could no longer hide as "wine with dinner." As crazy as it is to write this now, all of this sounded like such a relief compared to the feelings I had at the time. I didn't know what exactly I was feeling, because it was all a jumbled mess, but I knew it was heavy. It inundated me, and I felt terrible almost all day every day. I didn't know why or what specifically about the girls or the situation was causing it; I didn't even have the wherewithal to understand that I was suffering. I just had it in my mind that those street people had it better than I did, and whatever feelings they might have had were better than what I was feeling. And that looked like freedom for me; it felt like being an albatross at sea for months or even years.

Maybe sensing this or just wanting peace at home, Lindsey suggested that I get out each Sunday and drive north to Marin County for a run. There is a well-known farmers' market at the Frank Lloyd Wright–designed Civic Center, endless miles of trails to run and hike, and a little shop on a back country road where I bought farm-fresh eggs. These trips to Marin County went on for months. I know this because I can recall the seasonality of the hills I would run: The dry dust rustled up by my shoes during the hot fall months is just as evocative as the mud on those same shoes during the rainy winter season. The California poppies were particularly mesmerizing, their hypersaturated-orange petals fluttering like moths in the wind that blew down the valley from the Pacific Ocean. But no matter how many times over however many months I took these trips, these breaks, they were never able to quell the turmoil within. Every time I left home, the inevitability of having to return squeezed me like a vise. I'd take the long way home, down Highway 1, from Olema, past Bolinas and Stinson, and then through the Mt. Tam watershed to Mill Valley and the city, for the same reasons I'd take the long way home from work, and it was just as unsuccessful. Worse, I'd begin to feel guilty for being gone so long. Giving me that time away was like a bad investment for Lindsey, one that seldom paid off in the form of my being in better shape when I returned.

The other thing about depression is that it manifests itself differently in different people. My mom sequestering herself in her darkened room is one expression and probably familiar to many people. However, one of the symptoms listed on depression checklists is "inappropriate or excessive guilt." Maybe that phrasing evokes someone who's hosting a party but feels bad that not every guest is having a good time. "Inappropriate or excessive guilt" might not sound, on its face, like depression, but imagine having thoughts like that all the time about everything. When I left for Marin County those Sundays, I almost immediately felt anxious about having to return and what would await me. This anxiety would pulse in my body for hours; eventually I would start to relax, but the minute that happened and I started to have a good time, I would start to feel guilty about being away. This tug-of-war between not wanting to be at home and the guilt of being away followed me all the time. Both feelings were excessive and counterproductive, and they left me feeling conflicted and drained. Neither being away nor being at home brought relief. When I did finally return home, I'd be at least as exhausted and irritable as when I'd left, worn out from the constant back-and-forth playing out in my head and heart. For some people depression looks like fatigue and sadness, but for me it looked like this; I guess I'd call it the automated creation of infinite impossibility. A break wasn't a break, but rather an opportunity for my brain or psyche to create endless competition between guilt and dread. The fact that the girls were getting easier to manage as they grew, at least compared to when they were newborns, did nothing to assuage my anxiety.

The nights were a horror, especially in those first few months. It was a constant cycle of crying and feeding, feeding and crying, and I started developing rituals that I thought would ensure getting them to sleep, as if hopping on one foot but not the other was the secret. Eventually, though, they'd be in their cribs, and eventually, after however many minutes or hours of soothing, suckling, rocking, or pacing it would take that night, they'd sleep. When the rest of the night's work was done, maybe cleaning, maybe some laundry, maybe dinner, I would fall asleep from the exhaustion of simply being me, of vibrating at too high a frequency for too many hours. But sleep would never last for long. By one, or two, or three in the morning, I would be awake listening for any sign that the girls, too, were awake, certain that any perturbation in their sleep meant hours of torture for me in the middle of the night and a completely derailed next day, one event leading to the next in an inexorable downward spiral with no bottom. Each time I fell asleep and dreams approached, a burning in my gut would follow and I'd be stung awake. I could hear my heartbeat in my chest, my skull, the pounding irregularity of it. Overlying the sound of my own pulse was the certainty that I was hearing the girls awaken in the middle of the night. *Was that Isa crying? Did Pia cough? Are they awake? I know they are; I can hear them. Or is it the boy in the flat downstairs? I can hear* something, *anyway.* But it wasn't the twins. Or it was almost never them, anyway. It was something in me. Some hallucination, or something the pain in my soul was telling my brain.

The nights were barely tolerable even beyond those chaotic first few months, though, even after the girls' evenings and nights became more predictable, more settled. Later in their first year, even though they were sleeping through the night, the holy grail for any parent of an infant, the anxiety and dread did not abate, not really. How many nights or weeks or months in a row without a disaster would be enough to calm my nerves? There was never an answer to that; these feelings had become like a hole without a bottom. I suppose that the number of normal nights could have risen to infinity and yet my vigilance would never have waned. The facts were irrelevant. How calm, healthy, and centered the girls were was irrelevant. How much help we might have hired and how many "breaks" away from home I was given were irrelevant. The thing is, you start to normalize this kind of anxiety when it happens so regularly. It wasn't a discrete trauma or a limited period of angst; it was just my way of life.

To those on the outside, it seemed like we were doing great. In fact, the girls were sleeping so well that Ruby, our night doula, essentially fired us. I say this in jest because she was still more like an intimate part of our lives than an employee. She said to us cheerfully one day, maybe a month after the girls had started regularly sleeping through the night, "Okay, guys, you really don't need a night doula anymore if there's no one who needs to be taken care of at night." She was right, but I had kept Ruby on all these months because it made me feel better. It didn't make my anxiety better, but her presence allowed me to feel like we had an expert around, and in my mind experts equaled control.

So out went Ruby, and in came Wilma, who would stay

with us for five years. From the Yucatán, she spoke very little English, but she did speak Spanish fluently and even some Mayan. The girls' first language would be Spanish, and to this day they are completely fluent. I know how this probably sounds, and I don't for one second take for granted the tremendous privilege of being able to hire help. In the midst of all this, I thought about my own mother, raising my brother and me without any kind of a partner, much less any additional help, but that gave me and all my hired help no relief. And I get that many people who are reading this might be thinking of their own experience and struggles and feel even more overwhelmed, since they aren't in a position to add another person to take some of the responsibility off them. But as I've said in so many other ways, the problem wasn't the work involved in caring for infant twins. Having Ruby and Wilma around, while they brought much to our family, including love, didn't actually bring me real peace or respite from my feelings. If anything, their presence masked those feelings further.

With this new daytime help, Lindsey started taking off for the trails of Marin as well. Once a week she'd meet her high school friend Laura at Tennessee Valley, part of the Golden Gate National Recreation Area, north of the Golden Gate Bridge, on the Pacific Coast side of Marin County. This remote and dramatic valley is named for the shipwreck of a gold-rush-era steamer ship, the SS *Tennessee,* that still lies underwater just off the coast. The smell of eucalyptus and the sight of bobcats underscore the wildness of the place. The Tennessee Valley Trail meanders between hills until suddenly you are smack-dab in front of the Pacific Ocean. Laura is a psychologist, but she's also one of Lindsey's dearest friends. It was on one of these runs that Lindsey started talking about me, not seeking a diagnosis but just venting out of frustration. I'm not sure if Lindsey even thought something was really wrong with me. Sometimes when you're in it, you just think this is your life now, or you're married to a grouch and maybe you should have picked better. But on that fateful Friday, in January of 2021, when she was describing a recent interaction between the two of us as they were running uphill and the hawks were soaring overhead, Laura said, "Maybe Chris has post-natal depression." Something about that line instantly clicked with Lindsey. She said later that it was like everything came into sharp focus. In rapid-fire succession, a blitz of thoughts went through her mind: *Oh, so this isn't normal.* And *My suffering being around him is actually suffering.* And *He has a problem; he isn't just a miserable human being.*

She was floored. She said to Laura, "What? Men get post-natal depression?"

"Sure," Laura replied.

"What does it look like?"

"The same as in women. Look it up."

Lindsey had barely shut the door of her car in the parking lot before looking up on her phone "post-natal depression in men." While it was similar to what happened in women who had recently given birth, some of the signs and symptoms were different. But the most interesting thing to her was that I had *every single one* of the signs and symptoms listed, even "psychomotor agitation." I had developed a nervous tic of running my hands through my hair. I was doing it so much that even Isa was starting to imitate me—much to everyone's chagrin, because often she did it while she was sitting in her high chair eating, and so got gobs of food in her hair. When Lindsey or Jenica or Wilma brought up my tic, I didn't deny that I was doing it, but I insisted it wasn't a tic; instead, I said, it just gave me a pleasant sensation.

Lindsey rushed in the door that Friday after her run with Laura; I could hear her footfalls on the stairs, heavier and faster than usual. I was in the dining room folding laundry as she came up the stairs and said, seemingly out of nowhere, "I know what's wrong with you!" We had never even talked about there being something wrong with me, except for that one stray-bullet comment about whether I'd been abused as a child, so her energy around this topic took me aback. I think that, much like her comment on our first date about a lot of women putting a lot of work into me, this was classic Lindsey: She was operating on instinct, gut, primal feeling. She was waving her phone in the air and pointing at something on her screen. "This! See here, you have paternal post-natal depression!" My first reaction was defensiveness, like, *Why do I have to have something? Why can't it just be that this is terrible and that's that?* It felt, too, like just one more thing to have to think about and deal with, another wave lapping over my face in an endless sea of waves threatening to drown me. And I felt pathologized, as if my feelings meant there was something "wrong" with me. But while I didn't initially perceive my need to control everything—a need that often felt ignored and intentionally unfulfilled—as a problem, there was no denying that I felt awful most of the time.

Later that night, when I was able to really sit down and reflect on what Lindsey had said, what her friend Laura had suggested, I started to have a sort of moment of warmth. With a very medical attitude, I thought, *If I have something, maybe there's a cure.* Medicine has no treatment for chaos; if it's "this is terrible and that's that," we're just stuck, and medicine has nothing for you. But if you have something, if there's a problem in you, one you can put a name on, well, maybe there's something for that.

I did a quick search and found a list of symptoms:

Depressed mood
Anxiety
Panic attacks
Inability to bond
Anger
Conflict with others

Drug use
Irritability
Risk-taking
Impulsivity

I had them all.

CHAPTER 7

THE ANSWER CAME LIKE RAIN, IN FITS AND STARTS

THE POWER OF a name, even one that merely describes rather than explains, is very real. We have lots of labels for things in medicine—some English, others Greek or Latin; some commonsense, others jargony—and they all carry power. They can define us and chart our destiny, lay out the next steps of our medical future, and give us hope for a treatment or a cure. When a bloody cough is just a bloody cough, it could be anything from nothing to impending death, but when a bloody cough is "tuberculosis," we know what comes next, and we know it can be treated. When tiredness is just tiredness, the mind reels with possibilities, but when tiredness is "iron-deficiency anemia," at least we know where to start, and when we eventually name the cause as "colon cancer," it's time to get to work on a treatment and a cure.

Our own names give clues to our pasts, our ancestors, our families, where we come from, and why we're the way we are, maybe even what we'll become. Rockefeller or Johnson, Singh or Lee—whatever it is, we know a little bit more by knowing the name. The name Choukalas refers to island people who fished. The names of our diseases might be even more powerful; they can categorize and divide, determine our treatment plans, inform us of our chances, help us find community. I've seen firsthand how many patients derive great relief from having a name for their experience, even if that name is just a name and not a cause, not a path to recovery or cure. Having a name for their experience may not mean there is a cure or even a treatment, but it means they are being seen, and there is immense power in that.

Despite all the time I'd spent around patients and diseases, I'd never given the power of a name its due. I'd thought of merely descriptive labels—like colic, which the pediatrician had suggested when I complained about the girls' crying—as meaningless. I'd always thought the relief patients felt from simply getting a diagnosis was silly, born of ignorance or denial. Cryptogenic cirrhosis? That just means we don't know why a patient's liver is failing. Idiopathic pulmonary fibrosis? Same, but for lungs. I recall sitting in meetings where very smart people were talking about some disease with subtypes A or B, and how maybe there's a third subtype that's a little bit A and a little bit B, and I thought, *These names and categories are meaningless; why do we even bother?* Even if they organize a set of confusing symptoms under one banner (as with colic in infants), I dismissed these names as not really meaning anything, because they don't provide an explanation or a way to make it better.

But then I got sick.

And I found I was not immune to that naming effect, the comfort it could provide. If anything, the name, the fact that someone had even come up with a name, meant I was not alone. Working from the small bits of information that Lindsey had found searching around the internet, we came across a handful of different names, from "paternal depression" and "postpartum depression in men" to "paternal post-natal depression," all getting at the same thing: In the transition to parenthood, men, too, can suffer, and that suffering can impact everyone around them, as well as their ability to love and bond with their new babies.

Not content with the limited lay information online, I did my own search on PubMed, a database of medical publications. Having a name provided great relief, but what PubMed wasn't able to offer was much real help. Typically, when I type a word or phrase into PubMed, it offers up sources by the hundreds, sometimes the thousands. If I don't immediately find quite what I'm looking for, I can add a term, or maybe take one away, and get another batch of results. But that day I found only one study. *One.* From the *Journal of the American Medical*

Association (*JAMA*), about a decade earlier, back in 2010. Those researchers used the term "postpartum depression in fathers." I also saw an expert-opinion piece,* written by a psychiatrist in 2019, describing the ways in which PPND and PPD (maternal postpartum depression) differ in terms of symptoms and risk factors. That was it.

The *JAMA* piece was a meta-analysis—essentially a statistical combination of multiple studies. It combined the results of forty-three studies that reported rates of depressive symptoms in more than twenty-eight thousand new parents, both mothers and fathers. It didn't define or describe PPND, but merely estimated the prevalence of symptoms in new fathers. Altogether, the researchers reported, around 10 percent of new fathers described symptoms of depression. They also reported that if one parent is depressed, the other is also more likely to be. Literally millions of men every year were suffering some version of what I had, and yet we'd never before heard the name in any of its various forms. But two decades into the twenty-first century, with everything we know about, well, everything, how could it be that there was so little on this, on me?

For starters, there is no agreed-upon definition of what

* The term *expert opinion* has a specific meaning within scientific discourse in terms of our level of certainty about the truth of something. In this strict scientific context, it is like saying a bunch of smart people who think about this stuff believe this is true, but our level of certainty about it is very low level compared to the results of large, well-controlled research studies published in peer-reviewed journals.

PPND actually is, or how to define it. It's impossible to study something if you can't categorize it and neatly define what it is, who has it, who doesn't, and how it differs from something else (and that's the real reason we have so many names and subtypes for diseases). Imagine wanting to study patients with strep throat. A culture swab of the throat is nearly 100 percent accurate at determining whether a person has or does not have strep throat. There are many viral causes of sore throat that can look and feel a lot like strep, but if we don't have the result of a throat culture from a patient with sore throat, fever, and malaise, we can't rule strep throat in or out. PPND is like strep throat without the throat culture; there's no test. Diagnosing and categorizing patients with mental health or emotional problems is often more difficult than it is for patients with "physical" or "medical" illnesses because to date there are no really definitive tests for ruling in or out particular mental health conditions or psychiatric diagnoses. There is no blood test for bipolar disorder like there is for diabetes, no nasal swab for schizophrenia like there is for COVID. Instead, lists of symptoms must be considered and behavioral criteria met, and often these symptoms and behaviors can overlap with other, adjacent syndromes. Sometimes it can take clinicians weeks or months to determine the diagnosis.

The expert-opinion piece from 2019, however, described PPND as a major depressive episode (MDE) occurring within a certain time frame after childbirth (either three to six months or one year, depending on the source). An MDE doesn't look the same in all people. The *Diagnostic and Statistical Manual of Mental Disorders* (*DSM*), the definitive catalog of mental illnesses, says that a diagnosis of MDE cannot be made unless the patient demonstrates at least five symptoms from among a list of ten or so—for example, depressed mood, markedly diminished interest or pleasure in most or all activities, significant gain or loss of weight, or sleeping too little or too much. The author of that expert-opinion piece got more specific than the *DSM*'s definition of MDE, positing that certain symptoms are more common in men than women, such as irritability, indecisiveness, and restricted range of emotion; other sources have suggested risk-taking behaviors, drug use, and conflict-laden relationship patterns as typical "male" symptoms.

The *DSM* has included maternal postpartum depression only since 1994, but it does provide a specific definition: an MDE during pregnancy or within four weeks of childbirth. Further, there is at least one validated screening instrument, the Edinburgh Postnatal Depression Scale (EPNDS), to identify and categorize mothers for the purposes of research. The scale consists of ten yes-or-no questions that assess symptoms such as feeling sad or depressed, difficulty sleeping, loss of interest in activities, guilt and self-blame, and thoughts of harming oneself or the baby. Still, these definitions may not capture the real essence of PPD and PPND. Nowhere in that list of symptoms was there a mother so delusional and distraught that she murdered her child, or a father so panicked he couldn't see straight, much less bond with his children or support his spouse. There is a sterility, a black-and-whiteness to such lists that doesn't even approach the universe of the lived experience. It's like reading about sex versus doing it.

Further, although the *DSM* has specific criteria for what constitutes a major depressive episode, making maternal postpartum depression and paternal post-natal depression sound more or less the same, my own experience has borne out what the expert piece suggested: that the symptoms of PPND and maternal PPD are different. Whereas PPD in mothers is described as being associated with sadness, guilt, and feelings of worthlessness, in men, in addition to sadness, there are symptoms like increased anger, conflict with others, drug use, irritability, violence, risk-taking, and impulsivity.

Did I feel sad? I certainly wasn't happy, but the word *sad* doesn't quite capture it. Did I experience guilt and worthlessness? That's not what stands out to me, not the way the anxiety and irritability did. However, the typically "male" symptoms were front and center. There were certainly anger and conflict; if anything, these were the hallmarks of interactions between Lindsey and me in those days. And my drinking had definitely increased (though it's also true that COVID lockdowns are known to have led to an increase in alcohol consumption in large numbers of people). "Wine with dinner" sounds sophisticated and within the bounds of cultural norms, but every night? That was new for me. And I'd returned to cigarettes, a vestige of my college days, smoking furtively on the fire escape, if only as a way to get out of the house and take deep breaths—deep, long, drug-laden breaths. I wouldn't have thought to check "yes" on impulsive behavior, but those long drives I'd taken had involved curvy roads, high speeds, and blind corners, plus I'd turned my car's traction control off. The lateral G-force of a too-tight turn paired with the perfectly timed downshift to blast into the straightaways certainly represented an enhanced risk of tickets, at the very least, and injury or death, at the most extreme end. Still, even at the time I'd known that I didn't want to crash and die; driving fast was more a way to escape the thought loop spinning in my head. If I was driving fast enough that all my senses had to be engaged, if even for just a few intense seconds, the pit in my stomach would recede and I could breathe. Still, whatever the upside, risk is risk. And in any event, the relief was fleeting: As soon as I was past the curve, the car's rear end snapped back into place, and the tachometer needle swung back below 3,000 or 4,000 RPM, there I was again, mired in that murky stew of unsettled feelings.

So I had all of the male symptoms. But where did all these symptoms come from? And why did they happen to me? These are tougher questions, and my deep dive into PubMed could take me only so far. But that didn't mean it couldn't be treated. Let me just slip back into my academic-medicine persona for a bit: While there are no specific evidence-based approaches to the treatment of PPND, because there have been no studies evaluating its treatment, we can extrapolate from data on maternal PPD. That data itself is sparse, for a whole host of good reasons: Pharmaceutical research in lactating women faces obvious hurdles, and busy, depressed mothers of newborns don't want to take time out of their chaotic, miserable exhaustion to participate in research. But as I once heard a yoga instructor say, we can only start where we are.

An excellent summary of maternal PPD and its treatment was published in the *New England Journal of Medicine* (*NEJM*), one of the most prestigious and rigorously reviewed journals in all of medicine, in 2016. The bottom line is that structured psychotherapy (in this case, cognitive-behavioral therapy or interpersonal therapy) was more effective than merely saying, "There, there," but the difference was small; still, more than half of patients in therapy got better over a period of three to four months. Because of results like this, psychotherapy is often the first thing caregivers and friends recommend. If the condition is severe or the patient doesn't respond to psychotherapy, medications like selective serotonin-reuptake inhibitors (SSRIs), such as sertraline, or Zoloft, or selective serotonin-norepinephrine-reuptake inhibitors (SNRIs), such as escitalopram, or Lexapro, are usually the next step. These medications are generally considered safe for breastfeeding mothers to take, as only small amounts of these drugs are thought to pass into breast milk (obviously, this is less relevant for men taking them). It's difficult to demonstrate that one medication is better than another, and, similarly, it's difficult to say one style of therapy is better than another, because no one has compared them for PPD. So, given what is known or recommended for maternal PPD, it is not unreasonable to extrapolate these findings to fathers with PPND, if only because it's all the knowledge that exists.

Darby Saxbe, a psychologist and researcher, has observed in her own research that changes in hormones occur at the same time as PPD and PPND symptoms (though we don't know whether this is a coincidence or whether there's some causal relationship). The simplest way to say it is that it seems like new fathers whose testosterone dips are more likely to be depressed. Although these findings are very preliminary, it would seem natural that various hormonal treatments have been attempted. Unfortunately, it can be difficult to make heads or tails of the research because the studies that have been done are frustratingly small and inconclusive. A number of other treatment modalities, such as transcranial magnetic stimulation, massage, and the use of nutritional supplements (e.g., omega-3 fatty acids, folate, S-adenosylmethionine, St. John's wort) have been tried, but little rigorous research has been conducted.

Since that *NEJM* article in 2016, two other summaries have been published, in 2022 and 2024. Like the 2016 article, both focus solely on maternal PPD. These studies echo the earlier review, suggesting that psychotherapy and SSRIs/SNRIs are the treatments of choice, and that there remains a lack of good data to support selecting one type of medication over the other, or one drug within a category; the choice often comes down to trial and error in terms of side effects. Electroconvulsive therapy (ECT), a treatment that is historically and socially, but not medically, controversial, was mentioned in passing as being an option for particularly severe cases, or those cases associated with psychosis, although no real studies have been conducted on the pros and cons of using ECT for PPD or PPND.

In recent years, brexanolone (an intravenous medication) and zuranolone (an oral medication) have been shown in good studies to be effective in women with PPD; both are thought to work by slowing changes in hormone levels after childbirth. Unfortunately, these medications have not been studied in men or in comparison to psychotherapy and SSRIs/SNRIs, so we don't know which is better.

Psychedelic medications, such as ketamine or psilocybin, have recently been described in the lay press as potentially effective treatments for depression and anxiety. In my own arm's-length experience as a clinician, I have observed improvement using ketamine in veterans whose depression has not responded to other treatments (though none were postpartum), and this observation is supported by high-quality research. (Anesthesiologists monitor patients undergoing ketamine infusion therapy, so although I was not the treating physician for these patients' mental illness, I would see and interact with them repeatedly over weeks and months, and the improvement was obvious.) No such studies exist for men or women suffering postpartum depression, and more research is needed; that might sound like a cop-out, but the medical literature is littered with early findings that look promising only to turn out to be harmful after more, higher-quality research is done.

To sum up what I found out and filtered through my medical experience, taking into account all the research done on things *adjacent to* PPND (because no one has ever really looked at men after becoming new fathers): It's clear to me that any type of psychotherapy is better than doing nothing, and if that's not enough, combining therapy with traditional antidepressants is highly effective.

Having a name for what I was experiencing and finding at least some medical research was a huge relief for me, but obviously it wasn't enough. I needed to actually get better for Lindsey, for Pia and Isa, and for me. And that meant finding a therapist.

CHAPTER 8

MY JOURNEY OF A THOUSAND STEPS

I SAT CRYING on our front stoop, talking to Matthew on the telephone. I couldn't see his face, but his voice was filled not just with sympathy but also with capacity and strength. I was crying because by now, in February, 2021, for maybe the first time in six months, I could feel an ally in my corner, and could imagine the concept of safety, if not truly feel it in my bones.

By then I'd realized I couldn't keep going on as I had been. In fact, the prospect of seeing a therapist started to feel like a huge relief. It felt a little like when you've been holding in a lie for a long time and you finally have to let it out; although there will be fallout, the relief is worth the consequences.

Looking for a therapist had been an all-hands-on-deck operation, and took about three weeks from the time Lindsey and I first starting talking about my need to get help. I certainly knew a few, and Lindsey's friend Laura recommended some, but it was Lindsey's sister, Jenica, who found Matthew. She'd had her own experiences with therapy, and also had kind of a sense for people; she had, after all, intuited a match between Lindsey and me.

Before talking to Matthew, I had had a few brief phone conversations with some of the candidates, trying to figure out who might be a good fit. I knew right away that I wanted a therapist, not a psychiatrist. I had enough insight to know that my *feelings* needed airing, and psychiatrists, being medical doctors, generally focus more on symptoms and medications. Furthermore, there's a whole range of different types of therapists, with different schools of thought and different techniques, and from my experience back in graduate school, I knew I needed someone who wasn't oriented too closely toward cognitive-behavioral therapy (CBT), which—as the name suggests—tends to focus more on problematic thoughts and behaviors. I know myself, so I know I can very easily get trapped inside my own head. I also know that for me, "facts" aren't the problem; what I needed was to deconstruct my feelings. Interpersonally oriented therapists, the kind I'd been mentored by in graduate school, tend to be really in-the-moment with a client, addressing what's happening in real time in the session, in a way that I knew would help me lower my barriers; I thought also that the close attention required of such therapists to make it work would help me feel seen and heard, attended to. When Jenica showed me Matthew's website, there was just kind of a warm sensation in my gut, one of familiarity, of peace. That first phone call lasted for just a few minutes so that we could get a sense of each other. I knew I needed to be pushed; I wanted someone who wouldn't let me intellectualize and dance around the truth. I needed to know if he had that in him, because sympathy and understanding and a warm voice go only so far. I even asked him about his theoretical approach and whether he would "call me on my shit." Would he challenge me? Would he push me out of my comfort zone, emotionally, and not let me get tangled up in facts? I remember unleashing a torrent of tears, of fears, of what made my body ache all day and all night.

At the time, I didn't have any understanding at all about what was inside me; I just knew there was something in me that needed to be shouted in order to get it out of me. All of life's pains, seen and unseen, acknowledged and unacknowledged, gather and gather. It's like I had a swirling miasma inside me that I'd been constantly managing in some way. Now, though, I was in a new life phase, one in which I was responsible for children with needs I could only imperfectly grasp. I couldn't manage it anymore, and it all just flew out. Think about water as it comes to a boil. Under ordinary circumstances, the steam escapes, and the water temperature remains at 212 degrees. But if you put that water under high pressure, like in a pressure cooker, the steam can't escape, and the water just gets hotter and hotter. With Matthew, right away I had the feeling of being in an environment where the steam could get out, where the feelings could be attended to. I was desperate to get it all out of me, and I just unloaded everything all at once: More than five years of IVF. The trauma of the babies' birth. Surges of anxiety, dread, and exhaustion with babies in the house. The guilt and shame of feeling like a terrible parent and an even worse partner. And that was just the first phone call.

Taking a step back, it's also fair to say that we'd all just been through the first stage of the COVID pandemic, and society as a whole was in the middle of a major mental health crisis. A group of researchers in the United Kingdom found that during the pandemic, people with underlying mental health issues were having more symptoms and feeling worse. I could see how the constant sense of impending doom, the very real risk of illness, and the recognition that someone we know and love might get sick and die would strain even the most resilient among us. On top of that were social isolation as well as the polarization and politicization of health information.

Right around this time, the first COVID vaccines had started to be rolled out. I received mine as an early Christmas present on the morning of December 24, 2020, after pulling an all-nighter in the ICU during which not everyone survived. I remember getting a text message sometime in the middle of the night—while caring for a COVID patient who was on a ventilator, had been turned onto his stomach to help his breathing, and had developed sepsis—that I should report to the makeshift vaccine clinic first thing in the morning. For the first time in nearly a year, we could feel a few tingles of hope and optimism, even while society remained mired in lockdowns, school closures, and remote work. After I finished work that morning and got my shot, I waited the required fifteen-minute observation period, then walked back to our neighborhood and stood in line at the local grocery store, as stores were still limiting access. Phil, who managed the line, had become a familiar face (or voice, at least, behind the mask). He'd ask about how things were at the hospital, and we'd connect through our shared humanity. I was putting my life and the lives of my family on the line to keep people alive for another night; he was putting himself in close contact with dozens or even hundreds of strangers a day so that people could buy food and eat. When my turn came, I stepped inside. The market was cold, the light sort of a ghastly blue-white. The shelves were mostly full, although flour was always in short supply, as was toilet paper. Gone were the bulk bins and anything that required handling; signs everywhere admonished me to touch only what I planned to buy. Plexiglass separated buyer from seller at the cashier stand.

After walking home and putting away the groceries, I sat on the chipped terra-cotta steps of our stoop, under the cold sun of the winter San Francisco sky, and took that first call from Matthew. As the number 37 bus pulled away from the nearby stop and headed uphill toward Twin Peaks, I cried into the phone, hoping for relief, yet knowing that relief was still months or years away. But like the vaccine rollout, it was at least the beginning of something to hope for.

Matthew and I met, virtually, each week. When we moved from the phone to the screen, I could see his face; he had the soft expression of someone who'd seen some things in his life. Short brown hair, trimmed beard, slim build, probably about my age. Maybe looked about how I might look to someone if I'd gone on to be a psychologist like I'd planned. Initially we mostly talked about how awful my life was. He'd usually begin sessions by just watching me over the video link, not saying anything or asking any questions, waiting for me to start, knowing that what came out would be a fertile place to get underway. Early on, I would begin by recounting how I felt at night, the pangs in my gut, and the pounding in my chest. Or I'd express some grievance about how Lindsey didn't take seriously some wildly overblown concern of mine, or describe how I couldn't catch my breath after Lindsey proposed yet another family trip sometime in the future that would involve a disruption of the girls' routine. If I said these things to a friend, the friend might just agree with me, fanning the flames. By contrast, a good therapist might *validate* the feelings of frustration, but then explore the why, and probe deeper. Matthew didn't take sides, and he didn't just agree with me. Sometimes he'd ask things like "What do those feelings remind you of?" or "Were there other times in your life where that same sensation came up?" as a way to explore what lay behind my frustration and tension, what the root of the anxiety was.

What I remember most vividly about therapy is how those questions led to intense and intensive exploration of the past, of my own childhood: the things that went unsaid, the most primal of childhood needs that went unmet. I think it started with Matthew asking me about my own early memories of childhood. The first things that came to mind were snippets, snapshots of disconnected things that didn't seem particularly relevant. Stepping out of a car in a suburban mall parking lot and seeing one of those blue-sided, yellow-roofed Fotomats that were common back in the 1970s, where you could drop off film to be developed and then later pick up the prints. The front yard of a white-sided suburban duplex. Learning to ride a bike in a grassy area, sitting on a red upright bike, bought at a garage sale, with "Montgomery Ward" written in blue on the chain guard, being pushed by . . . lord knows who.

But that's the thing about therapy and a trusting relationship with one's therapist: Once you start getting into that headspace, other things come up. Choppy memories of being dropped off at a babysitter's or a daycare in someone's home, mostly just playpens in a dark basement. Wet diapers mashed in my face. Chickenpox going around. Had I been two? Three? I was old enough to remember it.

The deeper we got, out came memories that in isolation seemed random but together formed a pattern of feeling alone when having a specific fear. I remember being maybe four and smelling an unfamiliar scent outdoors, and either someone told me or I invented that it was the smell of someone having been shot. It was evening, and we had returned from somewhere. Dinner out? As I climbed down out of the backseat of a two-door car into the cooling, sweet summer air, crickets chirping, the last of the sun just a rim of light against the horizon, there it was: the odor of something foreign, like smoke, something innately sinister. Did I imagine that's how a smoking gun smelled? Gunpowder? Or that a recently murdered body gave off a certain smell? Who could've told me that? It was just my brother and parents and me. Did I mishear? Did I make it up? Was it just some stupid thing my brother said? Either way, it was nothing a four-year-old should have sat alone with, and I don't remember my parents trying to talk me out of it. But then again, I don't remember asking them to try, or even talking to them about it at all. I remember mostly being alone in those dark thoughts, sorting out in my own mind what was what, answering for myself the mysteries of the world around me. I've encountered that same smell from time to time since, and I'm always taken back to that summer evening at the edge of a cornfield, stepping onto that driveway and wondering who had died.

I also remembered, around that same time, having felt sick when the oil truck passed through our neighborhood, spraying crude oil on the dirt road that fronted our house. It probably sounds strange today, but back then it was common both to live on a dirt road and to periodically have a truck come along and spray some kind of oil onto the dirt and gravel to keep the dust down. I can see myself, huddled by an open window, clutching a yellow synthetic blankie, feeling nausea and abdominal pain, nose and mouth and lungs filled with the smell of oil, being concerned about being sick, and all at the age of three or four. I remember having a cut on my thumb once and using that same tattered blankie to absorb the blood, which, as it dried, turned from a brilliant red to a dark brownish color. When I think back on these memories, these times when I was afraid, what stands out is that I don't remember going to my parents with these fears. Did I go to them and learn they couldn't be relied upon? Did I not know I could go to them, not know that their job was to protect and soothe me at such a young age? Was I just wired from the get-go to internalize all these fears, to rely on myself? Or, perhaps more likely, did I have even at that young age a subtle, unconscious sense that they were stressed and couldn't or shouldn't be bothered? That they couldn't handle my feelings or needs? Or that my problems weren't big enough to be worthy of their soothing?

Then there was all the economic uncertainty after the divorce. I remember being afraid a lot, having fears of poverty put into my head by my mother's own stress and concerns. During her time at Honeywell, throughout the 1980s there were changes in the business, frequent protests (the company had an affiliate that provided parts to branches of the US military), and round after round of layoffs, each one creating more and more stress in my mom. As time went on, her fears grew and became more vocal and explicit. That the worst case never happened, that she always managed to make it work, is beside the point, at least when you're a little kid. You can only hear "There isn't any extra money this month, so don't ask for anything" so many times before you internalize that worry. Her worries became my worries at an age far too young.

Writing about these memories now, I don't pretend they are particularly illuminating or even especially severe; they probably come across as mundane, really. It's not like we were digging ditches in a war zone. People endure immeasurably worse childhoods, from abuse of all kinds to war and famine. (Although maybe a lot of those people lose their minds when their kids are born, too, should they live long enough to have them.)

I don't know what sort of memories would indicate that my childhood was "good" or "bad," though it strikes me as tragic that most of what I remember from my childhood are these one-off little memories of things that made me afraid. But as I visited and revisited these events with Matthew, I would experience aha moments, when something would click and, for just an instant, it would all kind of make sense. I'd get a warmth in my chest when something I talked about in therapy allowed me to see my current experience through the lens of past experiences of what therapists call trauma. The simplest, most compact explanation is that a childhood filled with uncertainty and fear inevitably leads to the need to control one's surroundings, and when that need for control is tested by the uncontrollable, chaos reigns.

For me, it meant that as an adult, I experienced my life as existing in an exquisite, untouchable balance that, when strained by life's challenges, by the presence of babies, imploded on itself, leaving me broken into a million pieces, with no guide for putting myself back together. Matthew helped lead me back to a different reality, through breathing, meditation, imagery, and focus. Perhaps *focus* isn't exactly the right word; it's more like *un*-focus, drawing my attention away from my thoughts and putting it onto something internal that I could control consciously, like breathing. Such a basic and elemental thing, breathing is, but sometimes controlling my breathing was literally all I could manage. Often Matthew caught me spinning out during our sessions—maybe he saw the screen bouncing in time with my foot-tapping, or he noticed that I was fidgeting with one of my shirtsleeve buttons as I slid seamlessly from one imagined consequence to the next, or he heard my speech becoming ever more pressured—and he'd guide me back to the basics. At other times, when things were getting out of control at home, I'd do it myself, listening to some guided meditations, systematic relaxation scripts he had recorded for me.

I've thought a lot about what therapy was like, and what about it was helpful. In those early days, it was simply being held, so to speak, amid my misery and pain; being able to express myself, to say the things that were hard, the things that I couldn't make Lindsey see were so important to me (even if they were just born of madness, of anxiety). I say "so to speak" because, of course, Matthew didn't hold me, not physically. COVID meant therapy was virtual, via Zoom; I only ever knew Matthew at a distance, in a flat, two-dimensional kind of vortex. Though we'd both been raised in the Atari age and had been introduced to computers in elementary school, we weren't immune to all the usual IT problems: weak Wi-Fi, frozen screens, bad audio, and inexplicably ending up in different "Zoom rooms." But we made it work.

To be honest, the fact that we were forced to have virtual sessions instead of meeting in person made it less scary for me to start therapy. To put my academic hat back on for a moment: It's worth considering that this virtual phenomenon raises interesting questions regarding what it is about the therapy experience that makes people better (the data are clear that it does), and whether some or all of the benefit requires being in a room with another human. Is the sum total of therapy merely the words that are exchanged, the feelings revealed by phrases that leave the lips of the client and are reflected back by the therapist? Is it the techniques that therapists read about during their training—"If the client says this, try saying that"?

"Lean in, make eye contact, reflect back the 'feeling' words"? Or is it touch or the possibility of touch? Can the therapist see or sense things through body language or tone that don't translate well across the internet? Would a bad Wi-Fi connection make it difficult for the therapist to see a slight furrowing of the brow in response to an uncomfortable truth? Is there something physical that is transmitted, human to human, soul to soul, by means we don't yet perceive or understand—what some people call energy or vibrations? Is there a wavelength of energy we don't yet understand that connects us on a level inaccessible to the brain's cortex (and hence to our thoughts), one that is meant to heal? Below our awareness, is there some recognition that you are respected for who you are and that you are appreciated and understood, or at least supported, by another human during a time when you feel frail and desperate? Or that the darkest and worst thoughts and feelings that plague your insides can find air between the two of you in a space that won't generate shame and fear?

I asked Matthew about this once, how he thought therapy had changed in the virtual era, whether it had gotten easier or harder. I did not expect to hear that he had previously done psychic readings, having realized as a young child that he had a gift for feeling and internalizing others' energy. Over time, he had attracted something of a national audience, and—prior to the pandemic, when videoconferencing had become accessible to many people—some of his work with clients was conducted via telephone. He found that meeting via telephone allowed him to shut out a lot of extraneous "noise," and that the work was somehow easier that way. Sure, meeting in person meant there would sometimes be nonverbal feedback (the inevitable nodding or quizzical looks in response to his impressions) that is absent over the phone, but such signals were just as likely to cloud his senses as clarify anything, he said. For therapy, he had the same impression; yes, he might miss that a client had alcohol on their breath, or had a nervously tapping foot, or hadn't showered in days, but those things didn't capture the essence of effective therapy. Besides, he said, people miss their sessions way less frequently when they no longer had to drive to his office.

So, then, what *is* this thing that happens in therapy? How did it help me? How do we get from the words and the thoughts and the exercises to actually feeling better, to putting ourselves back together? Matthew talks not about sympathy but about sensitivity, or attunement—the art or act of, as he says, holding space compassionately. As near as I can tell, attunement is, in part, paying attention to the person who is suffering, and doing so selflessly and exclusively for their benefit. It is a heightened level of attending to subtext.

For me, it started with just having a person to talk to with whom I could be honest, from whom I no longer had to hide the things that needed to find expression, no matter how ridiculous, no matter how dark. I undertook directed introspection into my upbringing, and a lot of the memories of my early years were, in part, rediscovered during that introspection. It wasn't so much that I had forgotten them; rather, when I got into a therapeutic headspace, one where I could live inside the moving images of these memories, where Matthew was truly inviting it, two things happened. First, I could see details, granularity, that the years had buffed out. Second, I think I gained perspective on the circumstances of my childhood. I grew up a certain way, and however I turned out, that's all I really know; a therapist can help me place those experiences within a framework of how that might impact a person growing up, in adulthood, and ultimately in parenthood.

Matthew introduced me to guided meditation to help with the actual bodily sensations that pierced through the thoughts and feelings. He showed me how to create a meditative mood that fostered a less guarded state, one that made it easier to talk about difficult things. It's not just that being able to talk about them made things better; also, by giving air to those things, by looking at them objectively, publicly, I could find a new perspective on them.

Over time, my explorations become less experiential and more cognitive. Less crying, more homework. Certainly Matthew offered advice, interpretations, and techniques, but I don't think those were responsible for the bulk of the impact. We talked a lot about the post-natal aspect of my experiences, the unique stressors of fatherhood. Matthew says this was on his mind throughout our sessions. While maternal PPD is now a formal *DSM* diagnosis, PPND isn't yet one, and there isn't a specific therapeutic technique designed for either. And at some level every parent ends up having unresolved stuff from their childhood triggered; often specific issues come to the fore when the child is at the age that the parent was when the trauma happened. But what made my situation distinct was the immediacy of the troubles right after the girls' birth, the "post-natal-ness" of it all.

Central to Matthew's direction in therapy was working through some of the acknowledged risk factors for PPND, and one of those was being witness to birth trauma. It was around this time that I began to remember that during our hospital stay, I'd had my annual primary care visit, conducted virtually, on my laptop, from our hospital room. We covered the usual material for a healthy adult male, but we were interrupted by one of the girls crying in the background, which prompted me to share what had been going on the past few days. I didn't know my primary physician all that well, having seen her annually maybe two or three times up to that point, but I could see even via Zoom the shock on her face as I described what had happened. At that point she said, "This is birth trauma; you're living it right now. You probably can't hear this, but try. When things settle down, get to a therapist like your life depends on it." She was right; I couldn't hear it then. In fact, I didn't remember hearing it at all until months later, when unpacking the birth with Matthew.

It is at least in part how the relationship with Mathew made me feel that created the space for healing. I can give you the surface details: We are the same gender and the same age, and we both have divorced parents. There are a lot of other things we have in common, and maybe we would've been friends under different circumstances. Beneath all that, though, there's more to the relationship. I felt on a deep level that I could be myself with him, could share the deepest and darkest things, and it wouldn't scare him to know those things, wouldn't cause him to abandon me. I never had to be alone in those dark feelings the way I felt I was with Lindsey; I had leaned enough on her, had put enough of the weight of my anxiety on her, and she'd had enough. The day might come when she might really know me, but not until I had a better handle on it myself.

Matthew would blend therapy with what he'd call "woo-woo," things like hypnosis or astrology, tools from his own personal explorations, but beyond all that, the experience of being with him felt a lot like love, like friendship. Like intimacy. And even across Wi-Fi, his attention and strength made me feel like I was being held even as I shed tears, tears that brought a wave of relief, of release, without any fear or threat to my manhood. At the same time, the vulnerability I felt then, the very real sensation that I was drowning and needed help, made it not just easier but essential to do this kind of work, to be as honest and raw and open as I could be. Because if I couldn't get it right, if I couldn't get better, I felt like I'd lose everything.

Attunement also meant that he might see different subtext in the same behavior at different times. Early on, the subtext of my grievances with Lindsey was related to anxiety, but later on he dug deeper and probed the underlying resentment, tension, or conflict, in general, between Lindsey and me as another driver, a different catalyst of those grievances. Lindsey and I saw a therapist together as well, but only later; for now, it was all I could do to hang on for myself, and as much as she was hurting, too, she gave me the space I needed to work on myself.

A few months in, I came to be able to recognize better when the thoughts were intrusive and the concerns unrealistic. Matthew taught me how to use breathing exercises to lower my stress and anxiety (there is good scientific evidence they are effective at that), and I did them, but the feelings were still there, and the sensations in my body were still there. I decided I was ready to try medication, which meant I'd need to see a psychiatrist. Unlike psychotherapists, who might be psychologists, social workers, or sometimes even nurses, a psychiatrist goes to medical school and then completes a four-year residency specifically in the medical management of mental and emotional disorders. As a physician myself, and one with good insurance, I was surprised how difficult it was to find a psychiatrist taking new patients. Either because of COVID or because mental health is just generally undersupported, most psychiatrists had waiting lists that were months long. With Matthew's help, I was able to find one, a retired UCSF professor who had transitioned out of faculty practice and was seeing patients online only, from his home office. I felt lucky to have been able to jump the line this way; I don't know what others with fewer resources would have done.

Dr. Karasic, on screen at least, was a big, bearded presence, but with a soft voice and a kind demeanor. That kindness, though, is where his similarity with Matthew ended. It wasn't that Dr. Karasic was impersonal or cold, but the goals of our encounters were entirely different. Appointments were fifteen minutes instead of an hour, with a focus more on symptoms than on feelings. Whereas a good therapist looks at anxiety, for example, as something to talk about, to fully explore, to get to the root of, a psychiatrist might look at anxiety as a list of symptoms—Is the patient having racing thoughts? Trouble sleeping? Is the patient able to perform well at work? Is the patient using drugs like alcohol or cannabis to cope?—with the goal of figuring out which medication might best treat those symptoms. I remember taking the first 5-milligram dose of escitalopram, one drug in a category of antidepressants that had just been coming onto the market when I was in graduate school, and feeling like it was kind of a full-circle moment—something I'd learned about years ago at the moment I became interested in medical school and changed the course of my life.

Escitalopram and other related medications have a number of side effects associated with them, and when I first started taking escitalopram, I did have some nausea and a sort of vague unpleasant abdominal sensation that passed after a few days. These medications are known for typically taking four to six weeks to have any meaningful clinical impact, but after two months I still didn't notice feeling any different, even as I continued to see Matthew. My psychiatrist and I decided to increase the dose. I didn't experience any kind of before-and-after moment when I suddenly felt better, nor did I have any sense of elation or exuberance. Instead, there was just kind of a softening of my physical sensations, in the gnawing feeling in my gut in moments of panic. Over time I began to realize that I was having less and less of that panic-stricken sensation, and my extra heartbeats seemed to subside. I stayed on that dose for about two years, and only just very recently cut back down to the initial starting dose; time will tell whether I can keep coming down.

These medications are a central part of evidence-based guidelines for the treatment of maternal PPD—and by extension, in the absence of any data, PPND. For me, because family-of-origin issues and conflict ended up being such a big part of why I developed PPND, Matthew's psychotherapeutic approach targeting these issues was critical to my recovery. So in the absence of any therapy and medication regime specifically shown to be of benefit in PPND, I think what I had was probably as PPND-specific as was currently possible.

Once, after things were quite a bit better and I could be more reflective, Matthew asked me what I thought had been so difficult for me, what made me so anxious and afraid, in those early months of the girls' lives. My answer was that when you grow up the way I did, with all the worries and fears around even really basic things like shelter and food, to say nothing of insufficient love and nurturing, you end up trying to control your environment in many different ways. You develop systems to control the kinds of things that can happen to you—for example, being on time, not buying things that are going to wear out quickly, rehearsing conversations in your head so you can practice all the possible responses, having an exit strategy for when a situation might get uncomfortable. When the girls were born, I was faced with a combination of circumstances: Their crying ate at my soul; I was trying to meet needs in them that hadn't been met in my own childhood; the situation was uncontrollable, in that what soothed them one minute wouldn't work the next; and on top of all that, there was no escape, as I couldn't just leave and even being away from the house was rarely much better.

As I watch my own kids grow, I think a lot more about the interplay of nature and nurture. How much of any of this has to do with fate or genes or "wiring" or whatever? How much I can blame on my parents, or their parents? How did all of that lead to the fearfulness and sense of aloneness that I remember feeling as a child?

I think back to that memory of learning to ride a bike. Someone had to have been there, pushing me, teaching me how to pedal and brake, holding the seat so I wouldn't fall. And that someone was my dad.

CHAPTER 9

WOULD THAT THE APPLE FELL FARTHER

EVENTUALLY HE'LL DIE, I heard in different ways over the years, *and then you'll wish you'd done X, Y, or Z,* or whatever the thing was. *Send that announcement about high school graduation, college graduation, grad school, med school, residency, the wedding, the birth of the twins. You'll wish you'd reached out. Tried harder. Done more.*

Whose fault is it, exactly, that my father wasn't in my life? And does "fault" even play a role? I couldn't say. Maybe not being able to "say" was the larger problem all along.

Or maybe: Just fuck that guy. However you got to being a father, whether you like it or not, you're an asshole if you abandon your kids, and you can go ahead and get bent.

Besides, my brother did all of those things anyway. He sent those announcements, and he even visited our father once, on a work trip to Phoenix. The announcements went unanswered, and the visit, although followed maybe by a few emails back and forth, did not lead to any kind of relationship, did not salve whatever his years of absence had wounded in my brother.

I was five and my brother was six when our parents divorced. Too young to understand why, exactly, but I knew vaguely it was our mom's decision, not his, and I knew, too, that I was more stressed out when he was around. He didn't hit us and he didn't drink, but he had a temper and he was a yeller. I don't know what he was always so angry about. When you're a little kid, you imagine it's because of you, probably because that's what the anger seemed outwardly focused on, like the mess or our behavior.

What I know now as an adult about my own anger is that it is born of frustration, of unhappiness. Maybe my father was frustrated and unhappy with the choices he'd made, or just with the way things turned out. Maybe our mother was a pain in the ass. Whatever it was, Nick was angry and short-tempered all the time. When I was a young child, living with the brooding, the unpredictable temper, and the yelling was like living constantly under a dark cloud, unsheltered from the lightning and thunder. Maybe I never recovered. I don't remember being upset that he wouldn't be around as much after the divorce. I was five, after all, and probably not too insightful about my internal state, but I can squint a little and remember a general feeling that life would probably be calmer. I think I was frightened by the yelling and glad that it might be over. I remember being an older child and feeling that maybe it was a blessing that he wasn't around. More often than you might think, other adults felt compelled to express sympathy that our father wasn't in the picture. They seemed incredulous: How could a young man not miss his father? How could I not be sad or lost or half empty in his absence? At the time I didn't have the words to describe what yelling at and around a kid does to him for the rest of his life, how you become afraid of conflict and how that causes you to shrink, to want less, to assert less. To *be* less. I would often tell people we were better off without him, but that was only half the story. Yes, he was a terrible role model and we *were* better off without him. But the damage was done: We were different people than we would've been if he'd been a better father.

Was he some kind of a monster? That's always been the narrative, that leaving his kids and moving out of state was some kind of sin, and that was the story even before anyone knew he'd go more than thirty-five years without having any contact with us. With me. My own observation, or maybe my rationalization over the years, is that he was probably just some young, selfish dude, something to which I could easily relate. Had he even wanted kids? For Christ's sake, he'd been in his early twenties when we were born; at that age, how could he have known anything about what he really wanted? About what kind of life was possible for someone in his position, with no college degree, driving long-haul bus routes for a living? I know when I was his age, I sure didn't know what I wanted. I spent my early twenties nominally in graduate school, but more than anything I spent those years crisscrossing the great prairies of the upper Midwest: grad school, a girl back home, following bar bands like Martin Zellar's and the others my brother introduced me to from town to town, howling at the moon, a little too drunk and a little too feral, and mostly just kind of lost in a sea of misspent emotion. So I get it. I was angry and I was a yeller, too. I'd thrown things. I'd broken furniture, the whole deal. Now add a kid into the mix, and "I wouldn't have been ready for it" is like saying a tree isn't ready to fly to the moon. When I was the age he was when we were born, I didn't have a pot to piss in, much less the emotional maturity to do anything for anyone but myself—or even for myself, for that matter. I barely wanted kids even in my mid-forties, and that was after all my years of running around were long since over. I just think sometimes, who could blame him for not wanting to stick around? Like, it's not personal, as though I somehow wasn't a good enough kid or not worthy; rather, if you had an out from that kind of situation at that age, who *wouldn't* take it? When I think about my own angst and misery in those early days of parenthood, maybe I'd have left too if it hadn't been for the guilt it would generate. I "survived" my father leaving; maybe the girls would have, too.

But these are the rationalizations of a partially evolved

adult. As a kid, all you know is that he left and never came back. The sad irony, I suppose, is that all that angst in my twenties, all that withdrawal, isolation, anger, and drinking, probably came about in some way from my father's having left when he was that age. I've told myself and others over the years that I didn't need my father in my life, that I didn't miss him, that I did just fine without whatever it is that a young child, a teenager, a young adult, a man, and a father gets from having a functional relationship with his own father. I've said I don't think about him much, if at all. I've said that his behavior—his yelling, his ignoring, his absence, his abandonment—didn't affect me. I've said that his personhood—who and how he was—didn't affect me. But maybe it's all bullshit. One of the most formative relationships in a young person's life goes sideways, and everything's just fine? How likely is that, really? And whether it's conscious or not, that damage has a way of leaking out. It never stays hidden.

Guy Corneau, a psychoanalyst, published a book called *Absent Fathers, Lost Sons*. In it he writes, "Lacking a father is like lacking a backbone; an individual's psychological identity is like a spine. Lack of father is like lacking an internal structure." Is this why I don't relate as well to men, why I didn't want sons of my own? Is this why I spent my twenties loose, adrift, not able or willing to commit to anything or anyone? Is this, on some level, why I suffered through the first year and a half of my girls' lives—because I didn't have some kind of connection to a trusted human who'd been there before me and could help guide me through the worst of it? If I'd have been more whole from the get-go, more complete as a person, might I have been better able to withstand everything that watching your wife nearly bleed to death and then trying to parent infant twins does to a person? Or was it simply the unbearable stress of trying to provide something for my daughters, a kind of love and nurturing and support, that I myself did not receive?

I don't remember much about my father. His smell, or his voice. His height even, beyond that he was short for a man, and stocky; all his brothers were. I remember those weekend visits after the divorce in kind of a general way, always at houses that were a little bit too cold during the long Minnesota winters. I remember breakfasts making toast with Pepperidge Farm bread, ironically fancier bread than at Mom's house, and real butter from a stick, not margarine from a plastic tub. There was a cat—Sasha, maybe?—that belonged to his brother and roommate, Uncle Greg, but all I remember is that she would drool on my neck whenever I held her. What was wrong with that cat? Uncle Greg, like my dad's other siblings, stayed in our lives growing up, and although he, too, later fell out with the rest of his siblings, we'd occasionally still see him at the odd holiday here and there.

I remember my father complaining at a big family dinner once that my eating style (right elbow straight out) was bothering him. I guess I must've been poking him or something. At the end of one of those weekend visits, tucking us into bed at home, at Mom's, I remember him saying he'd "see us in a week." I had just started school and was getting used to a school week (five days), and so I asked, "A five-day week or a seven-day week?" For some reason that threw him into a rage. He yelled and yelled about what a smart-ass I was being. He just kept using that word: *smart-ass*. What the fuck was the matter with him?

There were better memories, too, happy memories, at least in the way that young children can be happy. Making spaceships out of the cardboard boxes from a new washer and dryer (which meant, I suppose, that there was money for new appliances). Playing catch in the side yard, him with his catcher's mitt, so worn as to appear decades old. And I remember, too, a long accordion-style hat rack mounted horizontally to the wall above his bed, with trucker hats from all the places he'd driven charter buses to for work—Estes Park, Colorado; Jackson Hole, Wyoming; Branson, Missouri; Chattanooga, Tennessee; and beyond. Mementos for him of when he crisscrossed his own prairies, howled at his own moons.

Something that really stood out are the multiple pairs of lumpy black work boots. Not cowboy boots, and not stiff rugged work boots, but mid-calf, slouchy, pull-on boots. The ones he'd polish and wear with so much regularity that now, more than thirty years later, they make the small list of things I remember about him. But aside from that, and whatever insidious insecurities from growing up fatherless are tucked away in my psyche, he's a ghost. I didn't randomly hear via other relatives what he was up to (he abandoned them, too); for all I knew, he might not even still be living.

But then the picture popped up and I wondered who it was, this person Facebook said I should know. Nothing in his face triggered any hint of recognition in me. We had one mutual Facebook friend, my uncle Greg. If not for the name, I would've scrolled right on past, but the algorithm doesn't lie: This was someone I was supposed to know. What a double meaning. To Facebook, I should know him because we're connected through the algorithm. But to society, I should know him because he's my father.

It was sometime shortly after starting therapy, maybe around eight months after the girls were born, and around the time I was starting to think a lot about the role he played in my childhood. Nothing about how he looked like seemed how I remembered it. The nose, the mouth, the proportions, the shape, nothing. There was something in the eyes I couldn't quite resolve. They didn't exactly look like how I remember his, and yet there was something there. The beard was gone, or different. Gone was the full Kenny Rogers chinstrap that I can vaguely remember from the few photos that exist from those early years; it was more of a goatee now, and all gray. His face was thinner, maybe, more drawn; more of a caricature? There was so little spark of recognition that if I'd seen him on the street, or in any other context, I don't think I'd have noticed him. Was it possible that it wasn't even him, that there was another man with the same name in the same town? But there was one thing that hadn't changed, not one bit: the glasses. Gold metal, not round and not square; I don't know the name for the shape, but I can see it in my mind's eye, with those lenses that darken on their own to shield against the sun and stay dark too long once you come inside. I find it ironic that it was an external thing, a thing that you'd think would change over time, be modernized, updated, that was the one thing that looked the same. Probably he still wore those same black work boots, too.

Anyway, there he was.

It wasn't until I went through therapy in middle age, in the throes of my own parenting crisis, that I could finally admit that his leaving impacted me, even if it felt mostly economic: The divorce meant we were poorer than we would've been, and that led to being ostracized in our relatively wealthy town. I remember paging through the JC Penney catalog late one summer, identifying a few items that I thought would be cool enough for the upcoming school year. *This shirt,* I thought, *will make me look and be just like everyone else.* I know how superficial and out-of-touch this sounds. It had to be about getting picked on for not having the right clothes or the right hair; it couldn't *possibly* be an emotional issue that had impacted me on a deeper level, right?

But come on. Honestly, fuck that guy. His anger, his yelling, his belligerence—all of that's in me. His anger fueled all my fears, my excessive need to fit in. Of course, simply divorcing wasn't the issue; leaving for Arizona and never talking to us again was. What did it feel like, I wonder, to pack up the apartment in the only town he'd ever lived in and move to Phoenix, thousands of miles away? And why there? Did he know at the time that he was leaving for good? Were there moments, after a few years had passed and he hadn't talked to us, when he'd be sitting quietly or lying in the dark and the thoughts would come in? In those rare moments when there wasn't anything else to think about, did he think about how much time had passed, and about what kind of person abandons his sons? Did he feel guilt or regret? In those moments, did he let himself feel ashamed, or did he let the next busy thought come in and take over, sparing him from those emotions one more time? Or did he somehow feel free, like we weren't his responsibility anymore, and whatever drove his anger and temper had been soothed?

I know now that people aren't just born abusive assholes. The expression "hurt people hurt people" is apt. As I've peered under the hood at my own issues and seen the parallels with my father's life, I can't help but wonder if my dad's dad was also an asshole and contributed to the way he was. This was the man who said he wouldn't shovel shit in the tux his son had rented for him to include him in his wedding, after all. And for that matter, what was my dad's dad's dad, my great-grandfather Nicholas, like? I sat down once with my uncle Peter, one of my dad's brothers with whom I've stayed close, to try to get some of that context, to try to understand where it all started, to understand what my father was like growing up, before becoming a parent. The stories were illuminating. My father, Nick, was the oldest of five, born to Fran, who'd emigrated from Greece, and John, whose father, Nicholas, my dad's namesake, had also. Great-Grandpa Nicholas had to lie about his age and stack lifts in his boots to enter the country; I've seen his name on the roll at Ellis Island. Contrary to what I'd imagined, my dad's generation had a relatively comfortable upbringing. Great-Grandpa Nicholas owned his own business, a dry-cleaning shop on what is now a tony street in a gentrified part of St. Paul, Minnesota, and his son, my dad's father, John, worked for him there. Some kind of conflict led John to find other work, in St. Louis Park, a suburb of Minneapolis that is tellingly distant from St. Paul. Peter told me that this was when things changed for my dad. Previously he'd been a good student, but after the move, his grades slid, he started associating with "ruffians," and the number of "loud discussions" between Nick and his parents increased. There was a lot of stress in the house. "Nick was a hitter," Peter told me, and Nick was always angry at something, though Peter couldn't say at what. John and Fran would yell, and Nick would yell back, and they'd get into shouting matches.

Even as a young child, I remember Grandma and Grandpa being yellers. They didn't yell at us, the grandchildren, but the house was just generally loud, sometimes in the fun, boisterous way, and sometimes in the scary, yelling way, and it started long before my brother and I were kids. More than once, Peter remembered shouting matches between Nick and their parents, and, Nick, in a rage, punching through the wallboard in the house. Peter came home from school once and wondered why a new Christmas decoration was hung in an odd place on the wall in the living room; he lifted it and saw it was covering a new hole left by Nick in what had been yet another round of fighting about grades and behavior.

But there was more to my father than his anger. He was a "clotheshorse," Peter said. He had a paper route plus another job, and so he could afford to buy some of his own clothes. (Too, sometimes things migrated from Great-Grandpa Nicholas's dry-cleaning shop to the kids' closets.) He had Gant shirts with the loop on the back, continental pants with the cinched waist. I even saw a picture once, maybe from high school, of Nick in a purple velvet suit. And he loved fast cars. He earned enough money to buy a red '67 Dodge, almost new, that he would take to drag racing events on the weekends to do the quarter-mile races. Peter remembered him once blowing up an engine and having the money to buy a new, bigger one.

As I sat listening to Peter talk about those early days, my thoughts drifted once or twice, following trains of recognition, distracted by sparks of familiarity, of connection. My dad was a clotheshorse? Well, so was I; in high school, I would save up my work money to buy dress shirts from Ralph Lauren, the ones with the polo pony and rider stitched in multicolored thread, almost photorealistic, on the left breast. I ironed them myself. That must've looked so weird, a fifteen-year-old boy standing over the ironing board Sunday nights before the school week started, obsessing over each little wrinkle. And he was a car guy? I remember that when I was a kid he'd always be pointing out some '38 Packard or an Austin-Healey, some stupid old thing that I never understood. We'd go to car shows where the old men would show off their old cars, which meant nothing to me at the time beyond the excitement of getting to sit inside them and pretend to drive. But then here I am as an adult, obsessing for years over the beauty and engineering of vintage Porsche 911s, enough even to own and drive one for a few years, and I've caught myself more than a few times pointing out old Porsches to the girls. After one pediatrician's appointment we even went to the Porsche dealership to poke around the new models, as if it were some kind of treat for the girls for tolerating the last round of shots, even though they probably couldn't have cared less.

And then there were the holes the adult Nick made in the wallboard of our home, plus a thrown boot in our apartment during an ugly fight with our mom over who knows what. I get it; I broke furniture in drunken fits of misdirected rage.

Whether it was nature or nurture misses the point; he's in me. He *is* me.

No matter how he became who and how he was, it has to stop somewhere, and if I've learned anything in therapy, it's that it has to stop with me. I can't fix him, and I'm not even sure how much I can fix me, but I can change the course of the future for my own children. I will not frighten my children, will not turn them into quivering puddles afraid of change, of risk. I will not abandon them, leaving a hole in them that they will spend their lives trying to fill, always in maladaptive ways, only to spend their lives not ever feeling like they're "enough." That will not be their fate.

For a few weeks after the Facebook suggestion, I debated with myself and others what it might mean. Was I being prompted by a mysterious force to try to reconnect with my father? "Honor thy mother and father," another dad said; he told me that it was incumbent upon me to take action, to reach out. Christian doctrine was never much of a pull for me, but I found it interesting how clear-cut this was for him. Most of the rest of my circle was more circumspect. And, of course, no one can really know how it would feel, least of all Facebook. Facebook couldn't know our history; it didn't even seem to know this person was my father. Was this some metaphysical signal, some ethereal call to action? Or was this the random output of a cold calculation by an algorithm unconcerned with its implications? I considered whether, against all odds, my crossing this decades-long divide could provide some semblance of a grandfather figure for the girls. I considered what the fallout would be if, like my brother before me, I did reach out and nothing came of it. Was it my pride that was at stake? Or would my cool façade of nonchalance shatter if I made the first move? Throughout it all, I couldn't escape one nagging thought: If Facebook was telling me that I was connected to him, it was also telling him that he was connected to me. Was he wrestling with the same questions, with whether to push the "send" button on a message of reconciliation, apology, or even mere inquiry? Or had he thought about it and made his decision, landing him on the wrong side of it yet again?

Those are questions that will follow him to his grave.

Even now the picture still pops up once in a while. One of those times I found myself staring at the eyes and thinking for a microsecond whether maybe, just maybe, those were Pia's eyes.

CHAPTER 10

IF ONLY I'D KNOWN THE MONKEY SLEEPS TILL NOON

As I write this, it's been four years since I started therapy with Matthew. The girls have grown to be able to fully communicate, and so have I. It's lighter inside the garage now, both literally and emotionally. The garage was where I'd sit in the dark, alone and afraid, after coming home from work, dreading what was to come. I'd wait as long as I could before going into the house, balancing my need to not be around the girls with the guilt and shame I'd feel for not "pitching in," for not "being a good dad and husband." That was where the darkest thoughts would come: Would I make it? Would they? Would I be delivered from this misery by the car crash that would take their lives?

But the garage is where I do therapy with Matthew now,

with the garage door open, so he can see my face. So I can see my face.

I do wonder at times what my mother and brother will think and how they'll feel when they read this. When they are confronted with how I feel about my early years, the way I was raised, and what it did to me. Will my mother feel like I blame her? I'm of the mind that everyone did the best they could, but the reality is that, for whatever reason, I needed something more than or different from what their best was. I don't know if it's anyone's fault; it just *is*. I can't go back and give my parents a better upbringing; I'm not even sure we can truly "re-parent" ourselves, to use the modern therapeutic parlance. I'm focusing instead on breaking the cycle with me and trying to give my kids the upbringing I think they need, or at least the one I think I needed. One of security, both emotional and financial; attention; and more or less unconditional acceptance and approval.

The work I've done begins to light the way for how I want to parent, what I think is important in my behavior around my children and my relationship with them. Something that feels really important and directly related to these insights about my own childhood is how I deal with their questions. Little kids have a *lot* of questions. Rather than minimize their concerns, I'm attempting to show them that they can trust me to listen and try to answer their questions when they are seeking help with something. It's fortunate for me that a lot of their questions are about the natural world around them, things that a person with a background in science can at least begin to explain. "Poppa, why does the earth turn?" asked Pia one night as I was just about to fall asleep next to her. "Why is the winter sun colder than the summer sun?" was another question. And "Which grows first on a tree, the flowers or the leaves?" I love these questions and could spend hours teaching the girls things that would help them understand. I wonder sometimes, though, whether the seemingly endless questions young children ask are really just idle curiosity, which is what they're often made out to be. I think it may be the child trying to make sense of all the unpredictable things they see in the world—an attempt to create some order amid all the new things they are seeing and feeling, an effort to quell the uncertainty that an unpredictable world engenders in them. I think back to the mysterious smell, the oil, the cut on my finger, and wonder how my questions were answered, how my need to create order from the unpredictable aspects of the world was met.

Still, as the girls have grown older, I notice that one of them, Isa, often seems to have a baseline of worry. Once she's strapped into her car seat, Isa wants to make sure someone is getting into the "driver chair." Here in San Francisco, the sight of driverless taxis made her think that *her* car could drive away with her all on its own. (To be honest, driverless cars make me a little nervous, too.) I notice as well that no amount of cognitive reassurance or rational explanation helps. It's not until I'm sitting in the driver's seat that she stops asking, and no matter how many times we get in and out of the car, she brings it up.

If I'm honest with myself, both of the girls are kind of anxious, each in her own way. Isa's manner is more direct. You can hear it in her voice when she asks whether I'm getting into the "driver's chair." With Pia, my mini-me, it comes out in her need to check things.

One day Ayn was driving them somewhere in our car, and as capable as Ayn is, it's a newer car that behaves differently than her own. Pia had a lot of questions and comments: "Does the car know how to get to tumbling class?" "Mia [that's what they call Lindsey's mom], the rain wipers are different from the headlights." "Mia, you have to turn on the wiper in the back of the car, too; it's a different lever." "Mia, do you even know how to drive this car?" Pia even asked me that last question the other day when I was driving. To some people it could sound cute; to others it might sound like she's challenging an adult's authority. But to me, it sounds like she's trying to soothe her fears, and that's something that deserves a lot of love and attention. Like with my own anxiety early on, there's probably no amount of "facts" that will quiet those fears, but I still think these things need to be met with compassion, understanding, and capacity.

I wonder, though: Did I do that to them—did they observe these patterns in me, or feel it from me? Is it just how they're wired? Is that just how I'm wired? What did my upbringing have to do with any of this? To be continued, I guess.

In one of our latest conversations I told Matthew how much lighter I was feeling. When I was first working with him, the change was cognitive, technique-y. I could do the thing—take deep breaths, meditate—but the feelings were still there. I remember telling him often how I wanted the changes to be internalized, to be what I actually felt, not what I had to talk myself into or out of.

In our earliest conversations I tried really hard, with varying degrees of success, to describe how the anxiety and panic actually felt in my body. What was happening in my mind was always easier to identify: racing thoughts, difficulty concentrating, memory problems, focus shifting from one thing to the next and one problem to the next, making a long and ridiculous chain of causation and dread. But in my body, there were sensations for which I could never quite find the words. The panic would start in my abdomen, where it felt like a gnawing. Strong at first, it passed like a wave upward through my chest and into my neck. Not sharp, exactly, and not painful, but a sensation you can tell isn't good for you. It would come on quickly, like an attack, and then although it faded, I was never quite the same afterward. Then there was the tiredness that came from enduring too many of these waves. As a physician, I know these words don't map to anything observable, or to any specific mechanism of how the body works that we are aware of. No one could draw a line from that combination of words to a specific anatomical or physiological issue or problem. If I didn't know it was anxiety and went to a physician to ask what was wrong, what these symptoms meant, the doctor likely would quickly become frustrated and dismiss these descriptions as being too vague and not connected to any diagnosis we understand.

It took a long time, but lately I've noticed that those feelings don't need to be managed with techniques, because they don't haunt me anymore. The inside of the garage is no longer a place of shame where I have to hide my face, but instead a place where I can celebrate with my therapist just how far I've come.

When I look back, I realize that two pivotal moments in my life—one when I was a child, and one in my development as a father—both took place at a zoo.

One of the zoos I visited in childhood had a smell that was equal parts seawater, fish market, and a sort of "animal" smell—a smell of something that is distinctly dead, but nothing in particular, just anything that no longer breathes or roams. I can still smell it, just like I can still see the little white wax-paper bag brimming over with cut-up fish parts, the guts soaking through. For one dollar, or whatever it was, people could feed the seals, tossing these cut-up bits of dead fish to them as they circled their aquamarine-blue donut-shaped jail at the Como Park Zoo in St. Paul, Minnesota. I can just as clearly remember that no way in heck was I going to touch those dead fish parts, no matter how badly I wanted to see the seals come up close and bark at me. But my parents would still buy those bags and feed the seals on my behalf, proof that there were at least some parts of my upbringing that were just for fun, that there were some moments of frivolity and lightness. The Como Park Zoo was an older, urban zoo, with small cages and cramped quarters. You can imagine a hundred or more years ago, when places like this were conceived, and animals like seals and polar bears were such curious oddities, like aliens in a land of squirrels, rabbits, and deer, that corralling them in pens for our amusement and curiosity seemed almost necessary. I was too young to feel sorry for the animals, and honestly never gave it any thought; I was just glad to get to see such unusual ones up close. We'd park for free on the street in a residential part of St. Paul and walk in, brown-bag lunch in hand because we wouldn't be buying food at the zoo. I don't remember much else, just the animals. Watching the polar bear do its obsessive-compulsive patterned laps, back and forth, touching its snout to the same spot in the corner on every lap with an urgency that even then was unsettling. Staring into the almost-human eyes of the chimpanzee, who probably had a name (the way Sparky, the main seal, did), as its lips moved with whatever it was eating. Could there have been a rhinoceros somewhere, too?

The other zoo of my childhood, the Minnesota Zoological Gardens (we grew up always calling it the "new zoo"), in contrast, was out in the country, with thousands of acres to create habitats for animals like camels and tigers and bison. Unlike the Como Park Zoo, it was built more around creating a more natural home for the animals, rather than maximizing the exploitative, up-close experience. I remember peering off into a distant field with anticipation, wondering if the camel or bison would be visible or hiding. Often they were hiding, and I'd feel disappointment. I would watch as the snow monkeys swung from branch to branch like the wild animals they were. And the Siberian tigers, their paws so giant and thick, their movement so silent, their colors unlike anything else in nature, and their comically large jaws—I wouldn't always get to see them, but when I did, it was like discovering gold. But the biggest thrills were the water animals. There were bottlenose dolphins and beluga whales that would participate in—well, maybe that's not the right word; maybe it's better to say that they endured?—feeding shows, where the animals would do tricks for food, jumping up and out of the water, dancing on their tails, or splashing the trainers. Mostly I just liked watching them from the underwater windows as they swam around and did their thing. When they came to the giant underwater window, you could almost think they were looking at you, looking you in the eye, as they passed.

I didn't ever consider how my parents felt about taking us to the zoo—whether it was easy or hard for them, whether they did it out of joy or obligation, whether they found it momentous or mundane. Knowing what I know now, it was probably a pretty big deal for them, or more likely for our mother, to take us.

Now jump forward several decades. I suppose the typical new father, one who didn't spend the first year and a half of his children's lives riddled with anxiety, wouldn't think much of it, but I was particularly proud of myself the day I took the girls to the San Francisco Zoo by myself. They were maybe two at the time, just old enough to squeal with delight in a way that let you know they really meant it.

The San Francisco Zoo was more like the Como Park Zoo from my childhood: small and maybe a bit cramped for the animals, but more manageable with two toddlers. Of course, the whole thing still felt incredibly daunting, but I knew, once I started feeling just a little bit better, that this was something I wanted to do, to prove I could. The girls certainly weren't asking for it, and I doubt they even knew that something called a zoo existed, but—I think because going to the zoo was one of the more memorable bright spots from my own childhood, and given everything that I went through, that we went through, in the girls' early lives—this was just something I knew I had to do. Perhaps as much for me as for them.

From conception of the excursion to execution was about two weeks. Two weeks to plan, anticipate, prepare, and worry. I plotted the route by car, investigated the parking options, scanned the food menu. Could I bring their collapsible wagon? Where would I change their diapers? Could I get there, have a reasonable visit, and still get home by nap time? Would they be too excited afterward to nap? If they had a bad night of sleep the night before, or woke up early, would I still go? I stopped short of doing a dry run in the car, but in my mind I walked through every possible obstacle. Lindsey was supportive, even though, for her, zoos were sad places where animals were held against their will. No matter; this was a journey I needed to take by myself.

I don't remember if I told the girls about the trip ahead of time; I probably didn't, thinking that if somehow I wasn't able to pull it off, they wouldn't live in disappointment—disappointment with me, this the first of many concrete promises I might end up breaking. I also thought it was possible they might say no, they didn't want to go; realistically speaking, they were two, so it's not like they had much of an opinion yet. Such rational thought, though, is not possible for someone with anxiety. The laser focus of worry will land on anything, no matter how improbable.

I don't remember how their night of sleep went beforehand, or whether breakfast that morning was easy or hard, or any of the usual metrics that would allay my anxiety. We must all have been doing well enough, though, because by ten thirty-five we found ourselves in the mostly empty parking lot, in plenty of time to get a good spot right up front by the gate. The sky was gray, as it often is in that part of town, close to the sea, and the beginnings of some mist were starting to form. It wasn't rain, exactly, or fog, but more a kind of vague wetness to the air; people who live here know what I'm talking about.

From the maybe fifty cars in the lot sprang families of all sizes, with a wild range of conveyances: giant strollers laden with snacks, toys, and the panoply of gadgets parents buy, hoping to make our lives with kids easier; wagons; bulky plastic push cars. For whatever reason, it was mostly dads. Maybe a nanny or two, and, inexplicably, some older adults who seemed to be there on dates, but otherwise dads. One of the fathers, shorter than me, Filipino American, and portly, dressed all in gray, as if to match the fog told me he brought his kids once or twice a month, and that they loved watching the penguins get fed. A couple of times a day, the trainers feed the penguins from big metal pails, and you can watch them inhale these eight-inch sardines, swallowing them whole. "Get a membership," he said. "You can come as much as you want." I asked him how old his kids were; he told me one was two and a half and the other was four. And then he said, "I don't know how you do it with twins, though, man!" People always say things like this. "Double trouble!" they say, or something equally inane and inaccurate (it's more like quadruple trouble). I usually stammer some platitude; "It's great," I'll say, "they get more fun every day, so many changes," et cetera, et cetera. But this time was different. Did I see something of myself in this other dad, in his tired face? Or was I just sick of putting on that false brave front? I don't know, but I told him exactly how I'd done it. How hard it was. How estranged and unconnected from them I'd felt. How terrible it had been on our marriage. How crippled by panic I had been. How I had lain awake at night, barely breathing, racked with chest pain. I told him so much that I finally had to stop, worrying that maybe I was causing a scene or that he'd flee awkwardly.

Instead he grew silent and looked down. "That sounds like me," he said. "Their mom had to take the kids to her parents' a few times. I was short all the time. She'd say I was angry, but I didn't feel angry; I just didn't have any patience for anything." When they were newborns he didn't sleep; he'd watch the baby monitor for hours, off and on, in the middle of the night to make sure they were still breathing. He never quite got over it with the first one, and then pretty soon the second one came. He didn't call it anxiety, or panic attacks, or PPND, but here was a man who had suffered, whose suffering, like mine, was still close enough to the surface that at the slightest hint that he would be supported, or believed, he'd tell a stranger at the zoo about it. He hadn't gotten any help beyond talking with his pastor a few times, but he said he was better now that they were older, easier in the ways dads find kids easier.

I think about that phrase a lot: kids getting "easier." Another one is "dads don't know how to relate to infants, but things get better when they're older." In the past I've thought that myself, many times, and said as much to others. But now it has started to bother me in the sense that it feels like it puts the burden on the kid to perform; "I can only love you, or tolerate you and your needs, when you can perform the right way for me, when these behaviors, interests, and needs start to come into the wheelhouse of what I like, what I'm capable of." I have wondered, too, whether I began to feel better because I was *actually* better, or whether it was just that the girls had gotten "easier" in the ways dads find kids "easier." Maybe that's looking too hard to find a problem where none exists, but these days I'm more careful when I talk about them and how we're all doing together.

That day we walked around a bit together, this dad and I, him with his kids-and-kid-stuff-filled wagon, me with mine. Not talking, exactly, but kind of just being there together. It was the first of a handful of encounters that taught me two things: People are mostly willing to hear what I went through and be supportive and not judgmental or shaming. And a lot of men, whether they know it or not, whether they call it anything or not, have gone through a hell of a lot when their kids are born.

That day, the real San Francisco Zoo—not the one I'd visualized with maps and pictures and mental walk-throughs—was, if anything, smaller and easier to navigate than I'd imagined. For the most part, I'd nailed it; there were no major surprises or hiccups. Still, with all that planning and prep, you might think I'd have become aware that monkeys like to sleep in. And so do the big cats. Like, seriously sleep in. By eleven thirty, they were still hiding away in their secret lairs, invisible to us all. But the penguins were out, and so were the flamingos, the grizzly bears, the snow leopards, and one mean-looking Komodo dragon. Certainly enough to keep the girls entertained, but I did have to do a lot of sidestepping around why they couldn't see any of the monkeys or lions, the two animals whose sounds they could mimic. "But I'm not still sleeping," reasoned Isa. "Yes, but you're not a monkey." "But Poppa, I *am* a monkey! Hooo hooo, heee heee!" Fair enough.

When it came time for lunch, I couldn't help but relive and overcome the experience of going to the zoo with the brown-bag lunch, something I had been weirdly ashamed of when I was a kid. It challenged some of the thoughts and feelings I'd had about my parents. I had packed some food, yes, but I had it in my head that I wanted to buy zoo food. Maybe I felt that it was more of a party if I bought junk food from the food court. Or maybe I felt like it was proof that money wasn't tight anymore, that I had "made it," transcended my own upbringing, as if that's what rich people did. I was probably expecting too much from the nine dollar fruit bowl, which consisted of slightly unripe melon, grapes, and out-of-season strawberries, as a totem of my psychological well-being, but we can be only where we are. Still and all, the fruit bowl was an adequate foil to the plate of chicken strips and french fries that followed. This gave me a moment of pause around my own parents' having had us brown-bag it. Could it be they had been thinking about something other than just cost when they had us pack our own lunches? Had there been more to the experience than my memory of it?

Something I'd observed a handful of times before had played out again: The girls seemed to prefer the healthy food I'd brought from home (beans, cashews, fruit) to the "fun" food I'd bought at the zoo. I've seen them turn down cookies for beans in the past, a parenting badge we never fail to wear. No matter, though; this was a *party*, and at a party you eat junk food. A little BBQ sauce here, a little ketchup there, and pretty soon they were chowing down on chicken strips and french fries like proper toddlers. Thirty-five dollars plus tax and tip later, there we were at an outdoor picnic table near the flamingos, eating lunch together as a family, just how I'd imagined it, how I'd seen others doing it. The sky had mostly cleared, and the sun shone through the vestiges of the morning mist, drying the slippery wet ground at our feet, and I tried hard to take a breath and focus not on logistics, not on next steps, but on the moment we were having.

It was really hard. It always has been, and continues to be, difficult for me to lose myself in something without the mental static of how to get there, how to get out, how to manage what might come, internally rehearsing each eventuality, each potential obstacle, each conversation, as if it were real. I've learned over the years that only by doing completely immersive tasks can I snap out of my head for just a few seconds. Snorkeling underwater, driving too fast in the car, road biking, and certain tasks involved in my job are some examples. But that day at the zoo I tried; I really tried. I tried to ignore whether they were eating enough, whether too much time was passing, whether there was or wasn't enough time to try again to see the monkeys, whether I thought the girls might still nap that day. I tried to focus on their smiles and their giggles, their requests for more french fries. I engaged in their excited chatter about the *gatitos* (in Spanish, the girls' first language, it means "kittens," but in this case they were referring to the fifty-pound snow leopards that were very clearly stalking the girls as a potential lunch through an inch-thick plate-glass window).

This mundane thing, having lunch with my kids at the zoo, was for me something herculean. Herculean not so much because of the effort involved in getting out of the house and navigating the million little things that can beset a trip with toddlers. Herculean not even so much in terms of the two weeks of planning and preparation leading up to it. But herculean in the larger context of my evolution as a parent, going from someone so defeated and disabled by illness to someone who could manage this thing and look, at least from the outside, like I was doing something routine, something easy, the way all these other parents looked. But then the obvious point hit me: Maybe we're all just faking it. Maybe parenting is (at least a little bit) hard for everyone. Like the father I'd met earlier that morning, maybe more of us are just barely getting by than we could ever know, could ever tell from the outside. Maybe just below the surface, many of us are bursting with emotions we can't quite deal with until someone has the kindness to ask, to share, to create a space safe enough for us to let it out.

I don't remember if the girls napped that day after all the excitement, but I do remember that for weeks they'd ask about the "flameengos" and when they could go see them again, and I could finally feel that sensation parents talk about: the reward that is so worth the effort. I did something for them that was difficult for me, and they were thrilled by it, appreciated it, remembered it. Lindsey couldn't have been more proud, and I loved how she was able to lavish me with praise when I had a victory like this. Beyond that, I'd connected with another father who maybe was suffering much the way I was—further proof that I was not alone, and for him, perhaps, proof that neither was he.

Looking back, I've wondered if it was really as bad as I thought at the time. I am smiling in the photos, yes, and I remember a number of mornings with the girls, just them and me, when we would sit on the floor as they'd roll around, play with toys, or just look at me and giggle. And of course funny things happened, like the time I was on my back, holding Pia in the air up above me, and she coughed up a loogie that went directly into my mouth. And not the front part of my mouth, from where I could easily spit it out; it went all the way back, like to the point where I was choking on it and had to swallow it. So, yes, there was "funny." But could I experience it divorced from the ever-present feelings of dread? Could I let go and just "be" with them without the nagging thoughts of next steps, of what-ifs? The truth is, I really don't think so.

CHAPTER 11

WE RODE AT DAWN

THE GRADUAL REALIZATION that I was not alone, neither in my specific suffering nor in the general fellowship of men, parents or not, has become a huge source of healing for me. The first inklings of that realization came in a weathered old coffee shop located by the edge of the ocean, which feels appropriate, as it was a life preserver for me. During the months of my worst anxiety and sleeplessness, I'd scurry to get up and out of the house, with the excuse that I was going to work, before the girls woke up and might need something from me I could not provide—whether soothing to stop their crying, getting them back to sleep if they'd woken up too early, or something I couldn't yet predict or imagine. I remember getting out of the shower, turning off the water, and praying that I would hear silence, each and every morning for months. Every time I got out of that shower I braced for a shock wave of panic, relaxing only after a few seconds had passed and I hadn't heard babies crying. Looking back, over the first three years the girls cried that early maybe twice. But every day I'd think about it, worry about it. As the months wore on and my insight grew, I was at least able to grasp how ridiculous it was that I worried about this every day, and yet the thing I feared had happened almost never. Again, though, the chasm between anxious worry and logic is as wide as the universe. And there were many false alarms. Sometimes the neighbor kid would already be up, yelling. Sometimes the floor would creak in such a way that it would maybe sound a little bit like Isa crying. Once or twice there was even a feral cat outside raising holy hell. Each time I felt the same burning shock wave of panic. Inevitably, though, the house remained quiet, I'd get dressed, and I'd sneak my way out of the dark house, sometimes in clothes that didn't match. I'd ease down the staircase, trying to keep from making the stairs creak—yet another opportunity to worry about waking the girls. But once outside, in the cold, dark, damp air, I felt free, as if somehow none of what had just transpired really existed, as if the girls didn't exist. I could breathe. The problem was, there was literally nowhere to go at that hour, around six in the morning, at least not where we lived. Sometimes I'd kill time taking the long way to work, but that was about as useless at soothing me as it was in reverse, on the way home from work. Sometimes I'd go to the ocean, park near the water, close my eyes, and try to work through one of those meditation apps. In the dark, I could see the lights of crab boats spread out over the water, out toward the horizon as far as I could see. I'd smell the scent of last night's beach campfires, still strong, a seductive reminder that life was still happening, at least here. I'd crack a window so that I could hear the waves crashing, thinking that all that energy, the force of all that water coming at me, would somehow do something useful for me. But it did not. Eventually, I found the aptly named Simple Pleasures, an old-style coffee shop, deep in the Outer Richmond, far enough out in the western part of the city that I could feel, hear, and see the ocean from the chairs on the sidewalk out front, and also get a great bagel and coffee. No modern glassy front, no blond wood, and employees wore rock and roll T-shirts, not hipster leather aprons like in the fancier neighborhoods. It was the only lit storefront on the block, or in the whole neighborhood as far as I could tell. This place was like a beacon for lost, lonely souls, the kinds of fringe denizens up and out at the ungodly hours before six A.M. The two Vietnamese men who bussed in from downtown every day before sunup. The occasional intoxicated street person. The French-Canadian photographer, always in the front booth. The respiratory therapist, smoking cigarettes in the parklet, the COVID-era innovation that turned street parking spots into wooden structures meant to give more outdoor seating, thinking maybe people could still patronize restaurants and cafes without spreading the virus.

That the place opened early easily made up for the worn furniture and the ceiling and walls stained with what was probably years of cigarette smoke, signs of just how long this place had been a neighborhood fixture (in case the nonworking pay phone on the wall wasn't enough of a clue). There were framed pictures on the wall of parties, open-mic nights, even a wedding. This place was in people's lives the same way people were in it. It was a place where people felt at home.

There was a silence, a stillness to the place in the mornings before the sun was up, like the dust wasn't even moving, like being on the edge of the earth or the edge of some frontier, before the crowd of more normal people would come through, people with jobs that start at a civilized hour, people who weren't hiding from something. It was the silence and stillness that I needed, a place to sit, breathe, try to calm myself, and be free of the fear and uncertainty of what was going on at home.

When I first started going there, the world was still deeply mired in the COVID pandemic, a time when sitting in a cafe was generally not allowed. I remember putting on my mask to go inside, following the arrows on the floor telling me where to stand, ordering through a piece of plexiglass, and then sitting outside in the dark, damp morning, mostly alone, underneath the warm orange light of the Edison bulbs strung up around the perimeter. Once it was light enough to see, I'd stare at the ocean, trying to meditate, hoping the phone wouldn't ring or buzz with a message that the girls were up early or that something was wrong, and where was I?

Over time, I met a few of the regulars (and even became one; a good portion of this book was written there), mostly men, some older, some with kids. A high school math teacher with a hundred kids a year. A line cook who had a daughter with autism and a son who later got into UC Davis. A truck driver for Recology, the trash and recycling company, whose son had special needs. A retired mining engineer. A retired architect. Some rich, some poor, one an artist who slept in his van, but all of them had experience and an ear. We'd talk about anything—politics, how the city was changing, COVID, and, of course, parenting. All of the other men who were fathers had kids who were well past the toddler phase, but everyone remembered; everyone could empathize, and everyone had survived it. Then came Carson, a married guy with young kids; I would eventually learn that he was dealing with some of the same kinds of things I was. I'm not normally very forward socially, but here was a guy about my age rolling up with his fifteen-month-old son, just a bit older than the girls at the time, and he looked like he had it together. I knew the second I saw Carson that I had to talk to him; I knew I had to make a connection to someone who could help me make sense of what I was going through, who could tell me that it gets better or tell me how to do it, or who might even have gone through it himself.

It didn't hit me at first how unusual and not-together it is to be out of the house every day with your toddler son at six in the morning. But as we got to talking, he quickly opened up and revealed that he had been dealing with sleeplessness, developmental concerns, and the stresses of marriage. Here was another man going through something, another man who could relate without judgment, without shame. Like I did, he found the fellowship of these unlikely men, in this unlikely place, to be an opportunity to heal, or at least to be heard and understood. Another man with something so close to the surface that he was just waiting for a receptive ear to let it out. This impromptu men's group had formed around us and gave us perspective, a set of broader shoulders to lean on, the realization that although suffering was a part of our lives as fathers, it could get better.

I've come to learn only recently that one of these men, the math teacher, lost his brother to heart disease right around the time we were all meeting and getting to know one another. He never said anything about it when it was happening, but then, I'm sure I didn't ask, consumed as I was with my own grief, my own suffering. When I found out, I apologized for not knowing, for not asking; he responded that he'd known at the time that I probably didn't have the capacity for anyone else's grief, but that now I did, and so he was finally sharing. Even if I hadn't realized I was doing a little better, others were paying attention and had noticed.

Time has passed, but I still get to that coffee shop a few mornings a month, right at the witching hour, right at six. The "Stand Six Feet Apart" signs taped to the floor have peeled and faded, the plexiglass is gone, and the paper cups have been traded back in for ceramic. Some of the men have come and gone, but many remain, and some new ones have joined. There's Adam, with two young boys, who sits and draws furtive portraits of others as he chats; there's George, the city investigator whose son is grown, but who remembers all too well the interplay of a difficult relationship with his now ex-wife and the son he was trying to shield from it. Sean, the contractor, whose son went to the local Catholic school (and whose other son, from a lifetime ago, remained in Ireland). And there are the runners, a group of Christian men, fathers, who stop in for coffee after their weekly runs and talk about their lives and their families. There will never be a photo of our men's group framed on the wall here at the coffee shop, but I feel no less a part of this community for the lack of it. Some places just foster a certain affection and bond, or simply attract the kinds of people who either need it or can give it. "This place saved my life," Carson later told me, and I knew he meant it. It saved mine, too.

The first big, early marker of improvement for me may have been the trip to the zoo, but behind the scenes, there were many little changes that were taking place as I began to recover: more time at home, more time solo with the girls, less time exhausted and debilitated. By the time the girls were two or three, I was still not truly casual about missed naps, perturbations in the schedule, anything out of the ordinary, but things were slowly getting easier. As therapy continued, I was coming to grips with what I had lacked in my own childhood and how that was manifesting itself now in me as a parent. The medication was also helping my physical symptoms of anxiety; I was seeing improvement in the burning feeling and the chest pain that I'd experienced for months. And instead of praying desperately for silence when I stepped out of the shower, I merely hoped instead.

Perhaps the most profound change I've noticed over time is the shift from leaning on others to having at least some capacity to have others lean on me, if even just a little bit. In the last year and a half or so I have become very open about paternal post-natal depression and my struggle with it. That so many others have found commonality with my experience and embraced my story warmly has been a recurring theme and, frankly, a bit of a revelation for me. I think these two things are interrelated. Instead of shaming me or judging me, I've found, people have really appreciated my openness in talking about it—in part, I think, because everyone seems to know someone who has a story like mine. "I think my husband had this," or "That sounds like me"—I've heard those comments more times than I can count. I had a colleague as a patient around this time; she and her husband had a five-month-old at home.

In our pre-op visit, before she was taken to the operating room, we chatted a bit, and I acknowledged how hard caring for a new baby was for me and can be for any man. Her husband thanked me for saying that, and I went on with the business of caring for his wife. The next day, when I called my colleague to check up on her, she mentioned how much her husband had appreciated my comments; she acknowledged that he, too, was probably suffering from PPND, and asked how I dealt with it. I shared a little more of my story and a few of the things that I had found helpful.

There was a long period when the girls were around two that I would come home from work and take them to the playground by myself most afternoons. We'd walk to the market on the way to pick up some nuts or fruit, something fun to snack on. We'd see Phil, the guy who'd always monitored the line during those early COVID months. His face now uncovered, he'd see the girls and smile; usually he'd offer me some kind parenting platitude about twins, or girls, or he'd comment on their cute outfits or whatever, and usually he'd offer them cookies. I'd bet my life he didn't remember me as the one jabbering away with him in those early morning lines so many months before, when I was just glad to be standing there talking to another human in the midst of so much chaos, both global and personal, instead of going home. But I remember.

We'd continue on to the playground in the Panhandle, past the Buddha Kitty shop, with all the oddities like the golden-colored, paw-waving cat statues in the window, where the girls would inevitably want to stop and look. They'd name all the little animal statues in English and Spanish, the turtles, elephants, cats, and more. After I finally pulled them away we'd reach the fence around the park—a fence that not only held in the energy and exuberance of dozens of young kids but also reined in the anxiety of parents who needed to know their kids couldn't escape or wander off. The playground attracted all kinds, from babies in the laps of parents who simply needed to get out of the house, to toddlers like mine who were running clumsily about, to the older kids, who always seemed to want to run *up* the slide in a move that demonstrated both their physical prowess and also their complete, age-appropriate disregard for the younger kids waiting to go down. Just the other day, now years later, I saw Pia walking up that very same slide for the first time, and knew all was right with the world.

The girls would sometimes play together, but more often than not they would go their own ways. Isa seemed to have a knack for identifying the older, alpha toddler. She'd bring them an offering, like a toy or a snack, and join their group. This is how she learned to high-five and fist-bump at such a young age, from an older kid she had hustled at the playground. Pia, usually on her own, seemed content to climb things—rocks, ropes, whatever—and she never fell, not once. Noticing these things meant I was paying attention, that I *could* pay attention, that for at least those moments I wasn't completely in my head.

I met some wonderful other dads at the playground on those afternoons, including a couple of dads of twins. I sensed that one of those dads, Charles, was struggling a bit like I had been. We'd stand there, hands in our pockets, watching my girls climb and descend the slide, and his girls, a year younger and born premature, in their stroller, the sounds of the Panhandle a low roar behind us. Charles would laugh uncomfortably about some of the things his girls did, things like getting sick, not sleeping, fighting sleep at nap time, or any of the million other little things that are normal parenting stressors but which for men like Charles, like me, created outsized worry and despair. Charles and I became pals, and our families did some dinners together, but at the beginning, those first weeks at the playground, I found myself offering praise and reassurance, trying to normalize this or that for him. He never "bit" on the emotional part, never said anything about the anxiety he might have been feeling, but I think it was in there somewhere. I remember specifically laughing with him about how his girls were at the stage where they would put anything and everything in their mouths and it was making him very anxious; wouldn't they get sick? Being that my girls were a year older than his, I thought that hearing about my experiences with their upbringing, their stages, and their foibles, and knowing that I'd made it through them, might provide some perspective and reassurance for him. I told him about how much sand and dead-crab detritus the girls would put in their mouths on our trips to the beach at Aquatic Park for Lindsey's ocean swims—so much that you could see it come out in their poops. Crazy-making, for sure, but it never seemed to bother anyone but me. And enough time had passed that we could see it didn't harm them one bit. My twins were safe and had gotten through it, and, as it happened, they willingly eat crab now, so maybe he and his twins would be fine, too.

This, like all these encounters with others suffering, was marked by how easily men will talk about these feelings and worries if given the chance and the space. So many were just bursting at the seams with thoughts and feelings about what they were going through. These encounters when I could lend my ear or my shoulder, share my experience, were as much for me as for the other dad, an opportunity to convince myself that I was less anxious and more confident, more capable than in the past. An opportunity to say to myself that I had been there and worked my way through it. That although I had known such ugliness, it gets better. That I was better. What wasn't better yet was the damage I had done to my relationship with Lindsey. That would take more time.

CHAPTER 12

TRYING TO GO FARTHER, TOGETHER

THE SUFFERING I endured in those first two years of fatherhood was not in isolation, and if I've undersold just how bad this was for Lindsey or for our relationship, it has only been out of the delusional hope that maybe it wasn't all as bad as it surely was. I've said a lot in these pages about the unpredictability of the behavior of newborns, how it felt like it could all devolve into utter chaos at any moment, and how I attempted to use rituals to control it. I came to realize over time that Lindsey felt the same way about me. She spent an enormous amount of energy and emotional bandwidth dancing around my moods and behavior. She carefully programmed so much of our lives in such a way as to minimize the chances that I'd lose it. I'd been engaging in rituals and routines that I felt were so important to minimizing my own anxiety, and she was doing the same thing, in a way, to try to keep things as even and level for me as she could, so that I could be decent and tolerable enough to be around.

I should know how bad Lindsey had it; as I've come to realize throughout this healing journey, this is largely how I felt growing up, between having a father with a temper and a mother who was depressed. The sensation of walking on eggshells around people is not only just anxiety-producing in its own right, but it also does not allow you to be your truest, fullest self. Making those kinds of concessions to others comes at the expense of how you want to live, who you want to be. In Lindsey's case, it kept her from being the kind of parent and partner she wanted to be.

I spent many months being continually irritated at Lindsey for ignoring the things I thought were best for the girls but which were really for me, things I thought would placate the jittery agitation that defined my world. Coming home from wherever we were early enough for naps, or really just not doing anything that would interfere with their sleeping at home, at different times in their development meant barely leaving the house or the neighborhood at all. I found her seemingly deliberate ignorance of what I was trying to do, what I was trying to structure, maddening. How could she not see how important it was that they not miss a nap just so we could stay out longer, or finish the hike, have more fun, or whatever it was? How could she not get that if we didn't turn back on the trail, we wouldn't be on the road by X time and then home by Y time in order for them to nap, and if they didn't nap, then they'd be cranky all afternoon, and when they were cranky, then they didn't eat well at dinner, and then they wouldn't go to bed peacefully, which would cause them to wake up early the next morning, and on, and on, and on? It was so obvious; how did she not see it?

And when she wouldn't comply, I'd get huffy, short, and irritable, so it wasn't like the fun outing continued anyway. Yes, life with infants and toddlers is better when they're rested and fed, but my insistence was more to soothe me than them, and it created resentment for her. Not only was I ruining the fun she was having by trying to curtail it, but being around me in those moments was terrible for her anyway. Talk about a lose-lose situation.

Looking back on all this with honesty and compassion, I can see more clearly what it was like for her. As I've gotten better and emerged from the shadow of my own feelings, my own experience, I've been better able to see someone else's experience for a change. I know now that it wasn't just my absence emotionally but also the intrusion of my need for control, my anxiety, and my panic attacks that cut into the joy she found in parenting. My presence wasn't just "not a help" or not a positive; it was actually a net negative, worse than if I hadn't been around at all. Bedtime was often like that. In those early days, doing those things alone was a lot, but Lindsey says having my help was sometimes more like having a third child to take care of. At bedtime, I'd worry and complain about the pace of things, thinking that we'd miss the window, they'd get overtired, and the wheels would come off.

I'm also aware of the tension between us during her pregnancy. On the one hand, I was checked out in that I didn't outwardly share the joy, happiness, and anticipation of being pregnant, of expecting. On the other hand, I had all these demands about how she should conduct her pregnancy—which tests to subject herself to, which doctors to listen to—that were largely born of fear about what might happen if we didn't "follow the rules." For my part, I felt like insisting on what was considered proper medical care was my way of caring for the babies, caring for Lindsey; it was just like how I felt like my behavior around the girls' routine represented me caring for them. But that version of caring just made Lindsey feel alone and, worse, unprotected. What Lindsey wanted was a partner in charting her own path, in supporting her pregnancy the way she wanted it to be; what she got was someone insisting on the party line about tests and ultrasounds and due dates at least as much out of a sense of anxiety as out of a sense of what was actually medically necessary. You'd maybe think that my being a physician would've helped, that maybe in me she could see the human face of the dictates from her obstetrician. Instead, she saw me as one of the many heads on the multiheaded dragon of the medical-industrial complex, bent on doing anything and everything no matter how small the potential benefit. It's not that I pulled rank or stomped my feet, but the truth is, I often agreed with the obstetrician, and to Lindsey that felt like betrayal, because she had a sense of what was right about her own experience.

It's difficult to rely on a man who is not doing well emotionally. Even in our modern world, with our increasingly progressive sensibilities about mental health, at the end of the day I do believe a woman who is becoming or has just become a mother has a kind of animalistic, evolutionary need to rely on someone. When that someone she's seeking to rely on isn't getting the job done, she starts to lose something—respect for that person, attraction to that person, faith in that person, all of it. It's very different from relying on someone who, say, has a broken leg; when it comes to the initial stages of parenting, they can't really help with the *work,* but as I've said, the work isn't even the hardest part of it. Even with a broken leg, you can still be a partner emotionally. And so as time went by I continued to sap so much of her joy in being a mother, I continued to need so much, and it took a toll on her. *I* took my toll on her. One can only be patient for so long when the need is to parent twins, because there's simply too much to do.

There were fights. There were tears. There was contempt. There were the awful things only she and I could know how to say to each other. There were weeks sleeping apart. *Weeks.* And there were therapists. For both of us and for us as a couple, together. I'd be lying if I said our marriage still isn't very much a work in progress. If forced, she'd probably tell you she resented me—for being sick, for being this version of a man, for giving her this version of the parenthood experience.

Truth be told, I resented her, too. For all the terrible things she said those months and years. For holding me to a standard that was necessary only because we had children, something I wasn't even sure I wanted. But if I'm honest with myself, the chaos of children was just the catalyst for my crashing out and my need for intervention. If it hadn't been that, it might eventually have been something else that triggered it. This isolation, this lack of connection to people, didn't start and end with the girls.

I've wondered if I deliberately held back things from Lindsey, but I don't think so. I think instead I was hiding much of my pain from myself, so it wasn't something I even knew to share with her. Given the work we have now done together and separately, and now that I have been able to "let her in" some, she has shared her own empathetic interpretations of many of the scenes of my life that I had so solidly etched in stone in my mind. For example, I often have described all my early academic accomplishments as "falling ass-backward," in the parlance of my Midwestern roots—kind of accidentally ending up in the National Honor Society, being a National Merit Scholarship semifinalist, and being named to Phi Beta Kappa—but she sees something different. She sees someone who is alone, navigating the world with an overly developed and unhelpful sense of self-reliance and an unwillingness to trust anyone, all learned through years of not feeling safe with the parents I had or because of the way my early fears, questions, and anxieties were addressed. Of course there was a college counselor at a high school like mine, Lindsey says, and of course they knew about your grades, your test scores, your potential. That I was entertaining a school like the University of Wisconsin, Eau Claire, meant that either I was too stubborn to ask for advice or I didn't want or trust that mentorship, that guidance, because that on some level I felt like if I didn't do it alone, then it didn't count. When talking about when I was in grad school and was unable to get to a meaningful plane of communication with counseling patients, I've often dismissed a deeper context, saying that maybe by that point I'd already moved on in my mind to medical school and was kind of phoning it in. But, as before, she sees something different. She sees more of that same closed-off self-reliance; I wasn't really getting their experience, wasn't really seeing them, because that would mean letting them in, letting them see me. And when I talk about how I chose to specialize in anesthesiology, I've usually thought first about the immediacy, the hands-on nature of the work. She sees someone keeping people at a distance, afraid to have long-standing relationships with patients, where patients might come to depend on me, physically, emotionally, and more. But coming full circle, knowing myself better, I can see now that seeking this distance from patients' long-term needs wasn't and isn't out of an *inability* to care, but an inability to maintain any kind of healthy separation from them. The same anxiety that paralyzed me with my children's needs would've done the same with my patients'.

Self-reliance is a double-edged sword. The way I grew up made me capable and self-sufficient, but what if it also made me unwilling or unable to trust anyone, or to really let someone know me, or to really know someone else? To have the kind of intimacy that makes a marriage, or any relationship, feel safe, worthwhile, and strong enough to withstand the inevitable challenges of life? In fact, Lindsey will tell you the biggest complaint she still has about our relationship, even beyond the first two very difficult years of our lives as parents and all that entailed, is that she doesn't feel like she really knows me yet, that I really know her, or that I'm trying hard enough both to reveal myself and to find out about her.

Even so, it is orders of magnitude easier now than before for me to support her parenting vision. Thinking back to all the instincts she had and the decisions she made based almost exclusively on those instincts, starting with the very early ones regarding all the tests and things during pregnancy and her insistence about knowing that it was time for the twins to be born, it is clear that her confidence comes from something extraordinary; she knows how to be a mother and what kind of mother she wants to be. I am more resilient than before, of course, and I can face what comes without the immediate panic that was the hallmark of my existence in the past. It's not that I necessarily agree with her more, but now I just have so much faith in her. I like to think that therapy has made the difference, that something about digging into who I am and where the scars are helps to release them. In part, too, I've seen over the years that the girls are healthy, vigorous, robust, and adaptable. Pia's high fevers, the ones that kept me up so many nights worrying and wondering, have morphed into nothing. Nothing at all. Also, so many of the choices we might make don't have clear right or wrong answers. And, as much as I don't like to say it, it's true that some things just get easier over time.

As hard as this has all been on Lindsey, she has also been my biggest booster. She's been in my corner, acknowledging how far I've come, especially given where I started out. She was the one who first realized I needed help and pushed me to get it. She hired Wilma to provide the assistance we needed in order for me to have the time to be able to see Matthew regularly. When I was finally strong enough to bring the girls back home to Minneapolis to visit my family, on my own, she was the loudest cheerleader. Even now, a year after the trip, she tells me she's proud of me for doing it, with words and emotion that makes me believe her, *really* believe her. She was even the first to push me to write this book, and she found my agent. Most of all, she is still here all these years later, even though things are not perfect. But as is the case with my own recovery, our relationship did not suddenly get better overnight, the improvement certainly hasn't been linear, and sometimes it feels like we've still got a long way to go. We still get into it sometimes, like just the other week when we argued about whether I was engaged enough in something that was going on at the girls' school, and it started to feel like those difficult conversations during our fertility journey when Lindsey didn't feel like I was on her side—or that dinner discussion in response to the *New York Times* article a few years ago, when we were at our worst—that just died of uncomfortable silence. But we can stay in it, now, both of us, keeping the channels open, with honesty, to keep working toward a resolution. That's how I know we're better now at talking about hard things, though; that's how I know we're growing.

I've been thinking more about the albatross, adrift at sea in its quest for solitude, and how I am shifting to the phase where it returns to its nesting grounds, to its lifelong mate, finally comfortable in its nest, finally at peace.

CHAPTER 13

THE MAKING OF ME

EVEN BEFORE THE girls were born, and even before COVID turned my weeklong stints in the ICU into the grueling death matches they became, Lindsey was leery of the impact that kind of work had on our lives. I'd do a week each month, and by Thursday, she'd say I'd be grouchy, irritable, intolerable, the inevitable result of the ongoing stress of trying to do nearly impossible things in an imperfect system, the overlay of the sadness of my patients' circumstances, ever present. So once I started doing these weeks again after the girls were born, while still trying to juggle academic projects and the countless emails and deadlines such projects entailed, her concerns intensified.

When I first began working as an anesthesiologist, my focus was to be the best and to work the most hours in the hardest and most intensive environment in a hospital, the

ICU. And I was very proud of being in a teaching hospital where I was both a doctor and a professor, and of engaging in mission-driven medicine at the veterans' hospital, where I could take care of the sickest of the sick, people who truly needed and deserved the best. This was my personality. I wanted, needed the validation of those titles. But the limitations of my self-centeredness and how I was using it to not deal with what was underneath were fully exposed when I had to come to terms with PPND. Once I realized that what had gotten me there was no longer serving me, I knew some big changes were coming.

My outlook changed so dramatically in those first nine months of my children's lives that I just couldn't go back to my job with the same mindset as before. There could be no more physical sign of the positive effects of coming through the other side of PPND than changing jobs so I could focus more time on my beautiful family.

I used to tell people I slept very well at night knowing that I was doing something good for society, that I didn't have to think about what kind of insurance someone had, and that I didn't have to worry about how the business of medicine shaped how I treated patients. Truth be told, I also enjoyed being constantly challenged by complicated cases. Eventually, though, I came to realize that, on a purely clinical level, I had done all the hard things, all the difficult and dangerous things, and felt like I no longer had anything to prove. As I was starting to understand myself better, starting to feel better, I realized the love of those difficult things was no longer there, and I was holding on to a piece of identity that wasn't making me happy anymore.

Beyond the patients and the hands-on medicine, there were all the other things that were part of my career: teaching students, residents, and fellows; research; publishing papers and book chapters; speaking at conferences all over the country. Did I need to continue giving so much of myself to these things that had defined my self-worth, or was my self-worth becoming defined by something else?

So I started thinking about what might come next, and I started making phone calls to people I knew. Most people I talked to were surprised I'd ever leave the university for private practice. A lot of them saw me a certain way—too professorial, I guess, or maybe too high-minded or, yes, academic, to be satisfied solely with patient care in a private practice. I visited a handful of hospitals and practices and talked to a number of people who were very happy and content with life outside academia, something I never thought I would imagine. All of these jobs were in solely clinical anesthesia practices, where I'd be caring for patients directly, one-to-one, in the operating rooms of hospitals, surgery centers, and sometimes surgeons' offices.

There'd be no supervision or teaching of students or residents, no leading an intensive care unit, no research, no office hours, and no one inviting me to fly across the country to give a talk. I worried that finding happiness in private practice would involve daily compromises as I let go of those things. From the other side of this decision, now a couple years into my new practice, I can say with confidence that the job transition has truly been a parallel of my internal growth and evolution. Instead of it being a compromise, instead of missing those things, I revel in the freedom and clarity. Where I worried I would feel like I was changing who I was or what was important to me in order to fit into a new job, what I've come to realize is that those changes had already taken place, or at the very least were well on their way. I had been developing an identity that no longer needed those external validations of worth, and so those other roles and responsibilities, those other marks of so-called prestige, instead of building me up and defining what I was about, were instead crushing me under the weight of expectations. Shedding them, then, was not a compromise or a trade-off, but instead an act of liberation, one that has been so intensely positive that I simultaneously wonder why I didn't do it sooner and know that I was ready to make that change only when I was ready. I got here as fast as I could.

Instead of colleagues constantly trying to flex about their grant funding or their visiting professorships or whatever, I'm now surrounded by people who just want to get to know one another, talk about their last vacation, get the work done, and get home to their families. I didn't know I was looking to connect better with people at work, but I have found the open and welcoming atmosphere to feel really good.

Beyond that, I can look at my contributions to medicine and my specialty and say I have done my part. I have done enough. I *am* enough. Absent those extra things now, instead of feeling less worthy, I feel more worthy. Whatever prestige and self-worth was generated by my work at the university was more than offset by the extra hours, the huge part of my mental bandwidth the work took up, the deadlines, the guilt, and constantly trying to be "enough" for my colleagues. Furthermore, although now I'm maybe in the hospital more hours than I was before, the impact of those hours on my psyche is less, and when I'm home, I have nothing else to weigh on me, to take me away from the people in front of me. Is this what Ayn meant, all those months ago, as the "making of me," a man defining his worth and happiness by different criteria, by the adoration he shares, in both directions, with his girls?

Even though I had left academics behind, I still had one last invited address to give, one I'd agreed to nearly a year prior, on occupational safety for anesthesiologists, a topic I'd published and spoken on in recent years. The topic is usually a bit of a snooze, to be honest, as it encompasses a host of health and safety topics including exposures to operating room noise and stress, X-ray radiation, and substance abuse. But this time, after paying lip service to those sterile topics in the first ten minutes or so, I veered. I acknowledged to the audience of around a hundred physicians that this would be the last podium talk I would give, that I was leaving the ICU and leaving academics, and I told them why. I told them about the things I'd seen during COVID, things many of them, too, had seen. I told them about watching my wife nearly bleed to death on the table in the OR, something we've all seen in strangers at one time or another, but never in our spouse. I told them about the girls, and about my struggles, and about the work I'd done to get better. And finally, I told them that I hoped, if they'd struggled with the things our calling had laid on their shoulders, or from the things in their lives at home, or from the things they carried from the generations before them, that they could get help, that they could get better.

I'd given a lot of talks to a lot of audiences over the years, but I'd never been swarmed afterward by so many people who wanted to share, who wanted just to talk about similar hard things in the presence of others who cared. I shared with these people not facts I had gleaned from books and papers, but parts of myself. In response, I felt heard, accepted, and appreciated. It felt like a perfect ending puncuation to a thing I was leaving behind and perhaps an opening paragraph of something new.

From the hallway just outside Operating Rooms 4 and 5 at Marin General Hospital, where I now practice, I stare at the East Peak of Mt. Tamalpais, the highest point in Marin County, where Lindsey's father, Michael, spent so much of his life hiking, and I wonder. Was what I went through during Lindsey's pregnancy and after the girls' birth a random thing, like catching a cold? Like developing cancer? No, not really. Certainly that's a small piece of it, for sure, but I think it would have been significantly different only if I had been more whole as a person to start with, which I think would have started with a different childhood entirely, one where I wasn't abandoned by my father. I also wonder whether any of this would have happened if Michael had been around, instead of dying when he did; if I'd had the help and support and love of a father figure, even if it wasn't my own father. And I wonder how much of it was the inevitable outcome of witnessing the trauma that started my life as a father, independent of how I felt while I was growing up.

My children know me as their father. I'm someone they ask for and want to spend time with. They tell Lindsey they miss me when I'm at work. I am calmer now, more ready to be what they need, more ready to embrace and enjoy being Poppa. I acknowledge that there's been no silver bullet here, no clean happy ending. Are things better with me and the girls? Extraordinarily so. Are things better between Lindsey and me? Most of the time, probably yes. Has this been worth all the work, the hours and thousands of dollars spent on therapy? The only answer is yes; I had no choice. The way things were going was not living, not for me, not for Lindsey, and certainly not for the girls. A different question, one I had been reluctant to ask myself, is whether the whole thing has been worth it. Like, would I have been better off if I'd never had kids and never had to dig out from such a deep, dark pit? But I *have* asked myself, repeatedly, over the course of the years I've spent trying to capture these events and feelings for this book. And the answer has changed as I myself have changed and gotten better. The answer was, in the early days of writing this, a tentative one, one I think I was writing as much to try to convince myself that this all had been worth it. Over time, and each time I sat with this chapter to address this line, the answer has changed, became more certain, and more true. It has been a hellish hill to climb, a hellish hole to dig out of, so bad the words to describe it have taken on shapes in my head that could only be ugly, could only be vulgar. And yet I am happy. I am content. And I am at peace. And that would've never come on its own, no matter how evolved I thought I was before all of this.

What I was searching for among the ruins of the first year of our lives together has finally surfaced. As time has passed and my recovery deepened, and as the girls have grown, my ability to find joy and humor in the everyday has grown along with them. From potty training to bike riding, from teaching them to ski to just watching them explore their worlds, there has been such a wild abundance of love, laughter, and lightness that the contrast is almost unbelievable. I have delighted in Isa's early obsession with all things electronic (though, inexplicably, she tended to wrap the cords from those things around her neck) and in Pia's habit of wanting to recite to me lists of things she loved that day. One time I came home from work to eavesdrop on a conversation in which the girls were lobbying Wilma (in Spanish, mind you) to lobby *us* to get them bikes for Christmas. The other night Pia emerged from their shared room complaining that she couldn't sleep because "Isa is making noise and fucking around," and I have no idea where she learned that word.

I was at work the other night, having just finished my last case; I was turning in paperwork and chatting with some colleagues. I noticed that Gene, an outspoken technologist with whom I've really jelled, was staring at me, eyes bouncing back and forth between my chest and my face. He finally said to me, "Who is that guy on your badge? He doesn't look anything like you." Glancing down, I realized he was looking at a photo of me taken years earlier at the university, the headshot that was meant to show how professorial I was. That photo had graced dozens of posters and websites advertising all the talks I'd given across the country. I saw it upside down, of course, but what I noticed were the suit and tie, the conservative style of eyeglasses (they were just for show; they had no correction in the lenses), and the look of self-satisfaction on my face, which I knew had come from being trailed by countless students and trainees following me around over the years, something I thought was what I needed to be in order to be liked, respected, even admired.

"Seriously, Dr. Choukalas, who is that guy? You look like a totally different person!"

I started to give him the easy answer, the answer with facts, but stopped partway through, realizing he was seeing something real, that he was asking something real. What I wound up saying was, "Gene, I don't know who that guy is. That guy was a whole lifetime ago, a whole different guy. Before COVID, before the twins, before my world fell apart, and before I managed to put a sliver of it back together again. I look at this guy and I think he's me, because I don't know any different; I've been looking at that guy my whole life. I *feel,* at least, like I am a completely different person; I feel like a new me."

CHAPTER 14

SHOW ME SOMETHING PRETTY

I'M FOLDING LAUNDRY tonight, on a white stone slab on top of the washer and dryer, and it's mostly the girls' clothes; the house is quiet, save for the droning hum of the dryer. Their clothes are so undeniably theirs, and so evocative, I can't help but let my mind drift to times they've worn them, picturing in my mind's eye Pia in her bird dress, Isa in the blue-and-red linen dress, both of which I found for them in Spain. Even though they aren't yet picking out the clothes we buy for them, they do often pick the clothes they might wear on any given day. People talk about how, at a certain age, kids start forming an identity, and I think for me, the clothes they choose have been one of the first elements of that. Pia's things are mostly pink, with pajamas that still have the footies (tough to find, actually, for kids older than toddlers, but she insists). She has a hand-me-down fancy dress with photorealistic cats on it, just regular-looking house cats with that stern, detached look cats have. She'll wear it every chance she gets, most recently on their first day of pre-kindergarten. Isa's things are more varied in color, less overtly girly maybe, like with bears instead of unicorns; they're consistently one size bigger than Pia's, and her dresses must "twirl." And so here they are, at this moment in time. This is simultaneously mundane, in that parents everywhere have little kids with hilarious tastes in clothes, but also so fantastically out-of-this-world gratifying for someone who spent the first two years of their lives unable to bond with them. Gone is the stabbing, gnawing feeling of panic; what I feel now in my belly is a warmth that's the physical manifestation of my love and adoration for them.

Is this what parenting is now, holding items that serve as memories and thinking of the girls when they're not in front of me? If clothes are memories, I'd rather be holding the clothes they wore as four-and-a-half-year-olds than the ones they wore as six-month-olds. But now, after four years and all the words in this book, I think I'm done talking about me and my dark, hidden parts. I'd rather tell you a little bit about my daughters, how they've turned out, and our life together.

I could tell you a million tales: biking with them to the next town over for groceries, getting up with them in the morning to read books and eat cherries, or that stretch in early 2025 where the three of us were sleeping together in the big bed all night, with Pia resting on my chest, which she calls her "*pecho* pillow," and Isa writhing around in her sleep like a bobcat in a sack. In those moments I was completely free, truly liberated from the chains that held me back from loving them in their early months and years. I could also tell you about a million mundane moments of bedtimes and mealtimes, the two major elements of parenting young children. Or I could sum up this whole thing by saying that all the things I've worried about turned out to be nothing, and that Pia and Isa are resilient, adaptable, kind, sensitive, healthy, and happy. Whatever nap they skipped, whatever outing we stayed too late at, no matter how hard I worried—none of it ended their world. They eat like horses and sleep like angels. And tomorrow they could switch roles or become two other kids entirely, that's how plastic their brains are right now, so I have to appreciate and remember what I love about them every single day. Every goofy mispronounced word. Every time they latch on to my leg, rendering forward progress impossible. Every time they're brave enough to eat something new and unexpected (this week was sardines on toast). Every time they get into the backseat of the car and ask for "rock and roll" and to "make it loud." And every time they tell me, out of the blue, that they love me or they miss me—or every time they just call me Poppa.

This daily affirmation of love for my children is only in part based on my cognitive awareness of the passage of time and the inevitability of their change; it's based in part, too, on knowing in my heart what a luxury it is to feel this love for them after all I've been through. To be able to feel the freedom to just love and admire who they're becoming, to look forward to seeing them and doing activities with them, and to miss them when they're gone—there's just no other word for that other than *luxury*.

But luxury doesn't come cheap. It sure didn't for me, but I am stronger now because of it. If I'd never been in the position of having to examine my own life, to do the work in order to grow and heal, I'd maybe still be going through the motions, alone. Sometimes I feel like one of those people on their deathbeds who, when grappling with their imminent mortality, begin to realize things about their own life in ways that give them perspective and clarity. I've seen it a hundred times in real life in my ICU patients at the end of life. Recanting old feuds. Releasing grudges. Reuniting family. Understanding the so-called meaning of life. Developing or reconnecting with faith. These moments of revelation and reconciliation are beautiful. But for them this clarity, this understanding, comes at the end of life. I wouldn't say it's wasted, exactly, but I've come to feel lucky that my opportunity to climb that mountain and check out a new vista came at a point in my life when I still have so many years left to enjoy it. The truth is, I've come to see this terrible experience as an opportunity that has left me better than I was before, and I didn't have to wait until my deathbed to benefit from it.

All the work I did to dig myself out of that dark hole helped me to be a better parent and a calmer, happier person. But it's also helped me to be a better partner to Lindsey. Those gains have seemed slower at times, but no less real. When your head's not screwed on tight because of anxiety, you're just kind of managing every day in order to get by—to draw on an image I've used before, it's like trying to manage dozens of spinning plates over your head. When you're in a place like that and one of life's big stressors comes along, everything gets thrown out of balance. All those coping methods you've been relying on cease to be effective, and the only other coping strategies you can turn to are animalistic, raw, and desperate.

Only by doing the work—looking back, dissecting the events, processing the feelings—could I arrive at the why and the how of my feelings and behavior. And only by seeing it up close in that real and vulnerable way could I start to do better. It feels poetic and emotional, but it's made me who I am in relation to the chaos I grew up in. How I define myself now, that chaos and abandonment by my father in the rearview mirror, is the groundwork for who I am becoming in the world. As time goes on, I sort of chip away at those faulty patterns, making different choices for myself against my initial instincts, which at times are not great. That's the struggle of the traumatized person. Sometimes I think of it like *kintsugi,* the Japanese art of repairing broken pottery by joining the pieces together with golden lacquer, making a strong and beautiful product out of shards.

By sharing my story and seeing how many people can either feel some part of themselves in it—or, just as often, can feel it gives them permission to share some totally unrelated aspect of suffering in their lives—has connected me to a shared humanity I didn't know existed. I'm not a Buddhist, but I have come to believe through this process that suffering, either big and fast, like mine, or small and slow, is an elemental part of the human condition. If you look hard enough and you live long enough, everybody's got something. Nobody gets out alive. Nobody. But that suffering is often experienced in secret and alone. I have been fortunate to have been given a tremendous amount of grace by others, and lucky that I have been able to grow from all of this, but it only happened that way because I was willing and able to talk about it out loud. So beyond learning about PPND or parenthood or fatherhood, or what it's like to have a difficult upbringing and no father, the larger takeaway for me, and I hope for you, is that the sooner we come to realize that one of the few things we share is the inevitability of suffering, the sooner we can embrace this shared humanity and cut one another some slack. And maybe by giving grace to others, the same grace that I received at my lowest points, we can give someone else the breath they need to keep going. To get help. To grow. To climb that mountain. To take in a new vista.

CHAPTER 15

IF WISHES WERE HORSES

THE THING ABOUT paternal depression—or paternal postnatal depression, or whatever you want to call it—is that because we don't have a firm definition for it, it's impossible to count the cases and know how many people have it. The best number I can give you, based on surveys and one meta-analysis, is that 10 to 20 percent of new fathers have symptoms of anxiety or depression, although they're not necessarily severe enough to meet criteria for a major depressive episode and therefore PPND. What I can tell you, based just on talking to people in and around my sphere, is that as soon as I utter the words, and as soon as I get real about what I was feeling, the number of people who feel the same, or some version of the same, is larger than you'd guess.

In 2024, a colleague sent me an abstract of a study being

conducted to identify patients who might be developing maternal postpartum depression via the use of an artificial intelligence algorithm to screen huge amounts of text in patients' electronic medical records. The results are less interesting to me than the fact that such a study could've added men's records with the click of a button and yet the researchers didn't think to do so. Even in 2024, that men could have this is completely off the radar. In 2018, the National Health Service (NHS) in the United Kingdom introduced a program to screen for mental health problems in the male partners of mothers suffering from PPD. Although such an initiative wouldn't have identified me, because Lindsey herself didn't suffer PPD, it is at least an acknowledgment from a major national healthcare body that PPND exists, or that men can suffer during early fatherhood. How much this has helped is unknown. In another sign the United Kingdom is maybe a little ahead of the United States on the issues, in 2022 a well-written opinion piece in *The Guardian* outlined a few stories of PPND in articulate detail and asked why the NHS wasn't doing more to identify and help these men. I include a sentence from one of the stories here because it reminds me so much of my own experience:

> I never thought about harming our daughter, but I remember thinking that I might be better able to deal with the grief of her death than the responsibility of keeping her alive and trying to support my partner.

So who are these 10–20 percent of men, and why was I one of them? Well, as with anything, there are risk factors. Certain people are at increased risk, including those with a history of depression in themselves or in either parent, those in poverty, and those who early research is showing to be experiencing hormonal changes. But all this really means is that deciding who has it, determining how many people get it, figuring out how to study it systematically, coming up with a way to test or screen for it, and developing ways to treat it aren't simple. It's no wonder, in the face of this uncertainty, that many clinicians might not know that PPND exists.

Of course, even a clinician who's heard of PPND can only consider this diagnosis if the man in front of them is willing to admit he has symptoms. Even the word *admit* here is kind of funny, as if to imply you're confessing having done something wrong. Plus, men are stereotypically quiet about their own mental health. Whether out of shame, stoicism, or an ignorance of the language of their feelings, men are simply less likely to acknowledge to others that they're suffering, and the medical literature shows that they are consistently less willing to name their feelings as "mental illness" or to seek help or treatment for emotional problems. There was a terrific focus group study out of Australia that sought to understand better this phenomenon; the title of the article reporting on the study was "People Say Men Don't Talk, Well That's Bullshit." Men in this study shared a range of explanations for keeping their negative feelings or emotional needs to themselves, ranging from being shamed by friends to the risk of such disclosures impacting their work situations. Focus group members made self-aware distinctions, too, between these external signals and some of the "internal" obstacles, like not feeling worthy of self-care.

Still, even with that cheeky title as premise, at the end of the day most of the men felt like it was more acceptable to talk with other men about their emotional experiences only if they were not sitting face-to-face (that is, they found it easier while doing something like driving or jogging together), or if gathering to talk about feelings was paired with other activities more in line with social norms for men, like exercising. Regardless of the cause of men's reluctance to acknowledge or seek help for emotional problems or mental health, the reality is that such reluctance exists, and inevitably it leads to undercounting the number of men who suffer from this.

And I think if ever there was a place to start, in terms of helping men suffer less, it's in finding ways to draw men out so they can be counted. In the medical research paradigm, this is always the first step. Getting an estimate of the prevalence helps researchers (and the organizations that fund researchers) understand the scope and importance of the problem.

If you gave me $100 million and said to go fix PPND, my old academic brain would say to start a foundation to raise more money, in order to fund a university to build a research infrastructure, hire scientists, and go through the long, laborious process of the march of science until a "cure" is found. But I think it would probably be better, more immediately effective, to spend that money hiring a smart marketing company to build a social media campaign to raise awareness and get everyone talking about the problem, so that individuals can recognize it and deal with it.

Outside the strict and structured world of science, does it matter that we don't have a precise definition of PPND? After all, definitions often exist only to make studying something easier. Can't we know it when we see it? And anyway, whether or not there needs to be some medical discovery unique to the post-natal or parental aspect of depression in men is a fair question. On the one hand, I think men are far behind women in the larger social process of addressing their own mental health, their internal state, and the unmet needs born of gender roles in society, and so just getting men in to see a therapist, even if it is the transition to parenthood that lights the fuse, would yield a tremendous benefit to society and to them as individuals. On the other hand, knowing some of what goes on in the body—for example, what role hormonal shifts might play—could promote the study and use of medications that might be uniquely effective for PPND beyond or aside from the usual treatments for depression and anxiety. That was the case with brexanolone and zuranolone, pharmaceutical treatments for women with maternal PPD. Or perhaps there would be developments in novel approaches to therapy or the availability of therapy in the context of new parents' tight schedules or for men who have likely already gone back to work. Just lately, in fact, I've noticed that podcast ads for the online therapy platform Better Help have been emphasizing men's mental well-being. Surely the increased availability and flexibility of new therapy delivery systems would make it easier for men to obtain this kind of care. Having been there myself, I am certain that having in-person therapy as the only option would be a barrier to care for many new parents.

Speaking of that early research into hormonal changes in men after their partners give birth: In the summer of 2024, I came across a couple of newspaper articles in the *Washington Post* and *The New York Times* about the work of Professor Darby Saxbe, a research psychologist and professor at the University of Southern California, who's interested in brain function after the transition to parenthood. For an academic psychologist to draw such mainstream attention indicates just how novel and meaningful her findings are. I was fortunate to be able to reach her through the network we share. When we spoke, I realized her findings were, not surprisingly, even more comprehensive and interesting than what made it into the papers. How she got there is fascinating. She was studying how brain chemistry and activity change during the transition to parenting when she realized that it would be difficult to get enough pregnant women into an MRI machine to carry out a good-quality study (even though MRIs don't involve the radiation inherent in other imaging modalities, the optics are intimidating enough to discourage pregnant women from participating). Studying men, she realized, both would be logistically easier and would offer the opportunity to separate the body's changes during the transition to parenthood from the experience of being pregnant.

Her work focuses on changes in testosterone (among other, less familiar hormones) and brain structure and activity in men and women before and after they become parents. The interaction between fatherhood and testosterone gets the most attention, I think because the public has all heard of testosterone, but the relationship she found is not a straightforward one. Yes, new fathers with lower testosterone are more likely to be depressed, she says, but they are also more likely to be engaged in caregiving and to be closer to and more patient with their partner. And, yes, new fathers who don't experience a dip in testosterone might be less depressed, but their partners are more depressed and less satisfied with them. The fathers are also more likely to leave the family.

She posits that these findings might be the result of an evolutionary shift that affects our family environments. In the distant past, more children died just after birth or in their first year, and this reality meant that, from an evolutionary perspective, it was better for new fathers to be less attached to their newborns and partners so that they could instead go out and spread their seed (and thus their genetic material) as far and wide as possible. Now, though, because there are fewer significant threats to infant survival, what's more helpful is investing more resources in the few children a family might have. The ancient environment was perhaps better suited to high postnatal paternal testosterone levels; the modern situation, perhaps to lower levels.

This makes me think about the popular concepts of helicopter and snowplow parenting, gentle parenting, and a host of other effort- and emotion-intensive parenting styles that you can read about on the internet and hear being discussed by parents at the playground, and I wonder if I see parallels to how I looked to parent the girls early on. Was I a helicopter parent? In a way, I guess I was, although usually these terms refer to tending to children's behavior and development, whereas my focus was on the routines that ordered their lives (and brought me sanity). It's interesting to think of the rise of helicopter and snowplow parenting as just an outward expression of parental anxiety. To be honest, though, neither of these patterns looks all that appealing to me.

But applying Professor Saxbe's research to what I was experiencing leads me to some introspections. After the girls were born and I was so miserable, afraid, and depressed, presumably my testosterone would've been low; if that was the case, shouldn't I have been more engaged in caregiving and supporting my spouse? Or maybe my testosterone was high; certainly Lindsey was unsatisfied with our relationship and with my performance as a partner and father, and I wanted to be anywhere but there. Professor Saxbe's point, though, isn't that one or the other of these testosterone and behavioral patterns is set in stone, or that one is good and the other bad. Rather, the healthiest scenario might be one where testosterone and behavior might fluctuate to meet whatever demands are present at the time. Or perhaps there exists some happy medium. Confused? Me too. I think all this really means is that although there are interesting trends and statistical findings that relate to hormones and symptoms, we're a long way off from understanding the "why" and "why me" of PPND.

Like any illness, from bipolar disorder to colon cancer, the causes are inevitably a combination of genetic and environmental. So what were my genetic factors? Do my parents have depression and anxiety? In retrospect, my mother certainly seemed depressed. I don't really know about my dad, but based on what I learned about his passage to adulthood from my uncle Peter, and based on the kinds of unhappiness that seemed inherent in his anger issues, maybe he was depressed, too. And there were environmental elements, too, the result of witnessing the traumatic birth of my children. The big point here, I think, is that Professor Saxbe's research is just the beginning of what we'll hopefully soon know about men and hormonal change post-birth. As the academics are always so fond of saying, more research is needed.

But as I write this, I can't help but feel discouraged and overwhelmed. Change in medicine takes a generation. It's been forty years since maternal PPD hit the *DSM,* and yet many cases still go uncounted and untreated, many mothers are still in crisis. Forty years is simply too long to still act surprised and wonder how it happened, what went wrong. So I can't help but think that I have to make it my mission simply to bring this out into the world for everyone to see and consider. With publicity and acknowledgment come screening—asking new fathers how they're doing, not taking the socially acceptable "This is great!" answers at face value.

At the end of the day, we need someone to ask these men what's really in their heads and their hearts. In medicine, we call it screening, and it sometimes feels perfunctory and out of place. But we need to ask them in a way that lets them know that it's really okay to tell the truth. The obstetrician has an opportunity before the baby is born to at least create awareness about what could be coming. They certainly talked with Lindsey about maternal PPD, but never about what might happen to me. After birth, the most likely physician to see parents in the at-risk period is the pediatrician, who is focused on the baby and the mother, and rightly so. But that's who's in the room; that's who sees these men first, assuming the father goes to those early appointments (which I did). And that's who, if they're careful and watchful and patient and know about PPND, can screen, can ask.

When I was a graduate student in psychology, there were a lot of conversations in the literature about cultural competence. Basically, did a therapist need to reflect the patient in fundamental ways such as race, gender, and socioeconomic status in order to truly understand and be effective for the patient? Conversations around mental health get both tender and complicated, and in the end it may seem unwise to add yet another barrier to effective care. But at the same time, I can see how men might be more receptive to another man when it comes to being open and frank about what they're feeling, even in the context of screening for PPND. Certainly, as I think I've pointed out in these pages, my experience is that men will open up when asked. A pediatrician friend from the hospital, Dr. Chris White, started a men's group for fathers; the goal is support, yes, but it's primarily aimed at providing parenting coaching for fathers of young sons. Knowing Chris and the combination of warmth and strength he exudes, I can't help but think that if he had really asked me about my feelings in those early days, it might have made a difference, and I might've gotten help sooner.

Maybe we need a prominent male figure—an athlete or an actor, maybe—to normalize this for fathers: "If that famous basketball player has panic attacks when he thinks about his babies, maybe I'm not defective or broken or not a real man if I have them, too."

The thing is, we need to live in a society where talking

about men's feelings and mental well-being is more normalized, and this is much more difficult. Having an organization such as the NHS talking about it is helpful (although, as far as I can tell, the effort to screen men hasn't gone anywhere; they announced a screening program a couple years back, but it isn't currently part of their programming). When I sit and really think about it, a lot of what we need comes down to societal change. But we can only start where we are.

Giving a name to what I had helped me gain power over it, and I believe the same can be true if you or a loved one is among the millions of men every year who have a new baby (or babies) at home and don't quite know why they're so miserable. And although there remain many more questions than answers, know that help is available, if only men knew to ask for it. In case the very fact that you're holding this book (and made it all the way to the end) isn't permission enough, let me tell you loud and clear: Man, I get it. I've been there. It is *terrible* to go through this, but you are not a monster for not bonding with your baby, for not loving your infant, for feeling strange and estranged, or for regretting every decision you made that led to their birth. And it doesn't mean you won't be a wonderful parent. Make the time, find a therapist, and tell them the truth. All of it.

ACKNOWLEDGMENTS

That this book exists at all is a testament to the courage and strength of my wife, Lindsey Cimino, who was not only willing to expose to the world the darkest parts of our life, but also make the time for me to write this. She read countless drafts and, like in so many areas of my life, helped me to see things that I could not, often right in front of me. Her imprint is on every page. I owe Matthew Engel an immeasurable debt; that I ever became well enough to finish it and realize my full potential as a parent and spouse is because of his skill, compassion, and perseverance. My literary agent, Bonnie Solow, was a tireless advocate and adviser, whose wisdom and experience guided my every step, and whose belief in my vision for this book kept me on track. Matthew Benjamin, editorial director at Harmony Books, dug deep, helping me craft my thoughts and experiences into form, never afraid to challenge me with uncomfortable truths. Thank you also to everyone at Penguin Random House who helped out on the book, including Andy Lefkowitz, Diane Hobbing, Meghan O'Leary, Steven Boriack, Rachel Tockstein, Allison Fox, and Mia Pulido. And Jen Anderson at TextElevate provided such deep and insightful comments that I will be forever grateful.

And to my mother, Diane, who died unexpectedly as this book went to press. I have always felt that, despite how parenthood started out for me and how that exploration led me back to my own upbringing, she did the best she could. For leaving Nick, for maintaining close ties to family, and for a number of other sacrifices, big and small, some of which I may only realize after her passing, I will remember her with love and gratitude.

ABOUT THE AUTHOR

CHRISTOPHER G. CHOUKALAS, MD, MS, is an anesthesiologist in community practice, and a professor in the department of anesthesia and perioperative care at the University of California, San Francisco. He is board-certified in anesthesiology and critical care medicine. He lives (happily now) in Marin County, California, with his wife and daughters.

ABOUT THE TYPE

This book was set in Garamond, a typeface originally designed by the Parisian type cutter Claude Garamond (c. 1500–61). This version of Garamond was modeled on a 1592 specimen sheet from the Egenolff-Berner foundry, which was produced from types assumed to have been brought to Frankfurt by the punch cutter Jacques Sabon (c. 1520–80).

Claude Garamond's distinguished romans and italics first appeared in *Opera Ciceronis* in 1543–44. The Garamond types are clear, open, and elegant.